CLASSIC SERMONS ON THE APOSTLE PETER

KREGEL CLASSIC SERMONS Series

KREGEL CLASSIC SERMONS SERIES

CLASSIC SERMONS ON THE APOSTLE PETER

Compiled by
Warren W. Wiersbe

kregel
PUBLICATIONS

Grand Rapids. MI 49501

Classic Sermons on the Apostle Peter,
compiled by Warren W. Wiersbe.

Published by Kregel Publications, a division of Kregel, Inc., P.O. Box 2607, Grand Rapids, MI 49501. Kregel Publications provides trusted, biblical publications for Christian growth and service. Your comments and suggestions are valued.

Cover photo: Copyright © 1995 Kregel Inc.
Cover and Book Design: Alan G. Hartman

Library of Congress Cataloging-in-Publication Data

Classic sermons on the apostle Peter / compiled by
Warren W. Wiersbe.
     p.   cm.— (Kregel classic sermons series)
    Includes index.
    1. Peter, the Apostle, Saint—Sermons. 2. Sermons, English. I. Wiersbe, Warren W. II. Series: Kregel classic sermons series.
BS2515.C53   1995   225.9'2—dc20   95-7844
                                         CIP

ISBN   0-8254-3998-1 (pbk.)

1 2 3 4 5 Printing / Year 99 98 97 96 95

Printed in the United States of America

CONTENTS

LIST OF SCRIPTURE TEXTS

PREFACE

THE *KREGEL CLASSIC SERMONS SERIES* is an attempt to assemble and publish meaningful sermons from master preachers about significant themes.

These are *sermons*, not essays or chapters taken from books about themes. Not all of these sermons could be called "great," but all of them are *meaningful*. They apply the truths of the Bible to the needs of the human heart, which is something that all effective preaching must do.

While some are better known than others, all of the preachers whose sermons I have selected had important ministries and were highly respected in their day. The fact that a sermon is included in this volume does not mean that either the compiler or the publisher agrees with or endorses everything that the man did, preached, or wrote. The sermon is here because it has a valued contribution to make.

These are sermons about *significant* themes. The pulpit is no place to play with trivia. The preacher has thirty minutes in which to help mend broken hearts, change defeated lives, and save lost souls; and he can never accomplish this demanding ministry by distributing homiletical tidbits. In these difficult days we do not need "clever" pulpiteers who discuss the times; we need dedicated ambassadors who will preach the eternities.

The reading of these sermons can enrich your spiritual life. The studying of them can enrich your skills as an interpreter and expounder of God's truth. However God uses these sermons in your life and ministry, my prayer is that His church around the world will be encouraged and strengthened by them.

WARREN W. WIERSBE

A Fortnight with Peter and Paul in Jerusalem

James McGinlay (1901–1958) was a gifted evangelist
and Bible conference speaker whose Scottish accent and
humor endeared him to congregations throughout the
United States and Canada. He pastored Baptist churches
in Brooklyn, New York, and London, Ontario, Canada,
and published several books of sermons that demonstrate
his unique homiletical style, among them *Heaven's Jewelry,
Not Now But Afterwards*, and *The Birthday of Souls*. Dr.
Herbert Lockyer, Sr., called McGinlay "a born orator"
whose preaching was "unique and gospel-drenched."

This sermon is taken from *The Birthday of Souls*, which
was published by W. B. Eerdmans Co. in 1946.

James McGinlay

1

A FORTNIGHT WITH PETER AND PAUL IN JERUSALEM

Then after three years I went up to Jerusalem to see Peter,
and abode with him fifteen days (Galatians 1:18).

ONE EVENING ABOUT nineteen hundred years ago, our
New Testament friend, Peter was sitting alone in his little
home in Jerusalem, reading a psalm of David and sipping
a cup of tea before retiring for the night. He heard a
knock at the door, and upon opening it he gazed for the
first time in his life into the face of Saul of Tarsus, now
become by God's grace, the apostle Paul. Upon noticing
Peter's chagrin, Paul put his hand upon Peter's shoulder
and reassuringly said, "Don't worry, Peter."

> It's all different now, it's all different now,
> Through His great salvation, I'm a new creation,
> And it's all different now.

"Oh, I know," said Peter, "that there has been a
tremendous change, but when I think of what you used to
be and when I realize that in this very town, and on this
very street, there are widows and orphans for whose misery
you are responsible, I just can't help being a little nervous
lest you fall from grace and break out again."

Drying a tear from his eye and gripping the hand of
his new friend, Paul reaffirmed what he had already
declared, that he was a new creature in Christ Jesus,
old things had passed away, and behold, all things had
become new.

Peter, by this time, had regained sufficient composure
to say, "Come right in," or as we say in Scotland, "Come
ben the hoose."

So Peter, the humble, homely, uncouth, Galilean fisherman, and the aristocrat, highly educated, cultured, religious

9

Saul, sat down at the fireside and began a two-week vacation together.

What, but the Gospel, and the salvation it brings, can break down social, religious, financial, and intellectual barriers, and enable two opposites like Paul and Peter to become the best of friends. Talk about the Lions, and the Moose, and Elks, the Masons, the Odd Fellows, and the Orangemen, no greater and more blessed fraternity ever functioned on the face of God's earth than the fellowship of the redeemed. Black and white, red and yellow, oriental and occidental, all washed in the blood of the Lamb. Won't it be a wonderful day when in Christ Jesus, "man to man the world o'er, shall brothers be for a' that"? Come with me and listen in for a little while to:

Their First Conversation Together

Without indulging the speculative or imaginative we can be reasonably sure that the conversation of these two men centered in and around Christ. Subsequent to Paul's conversion and prior to the commencement of his public ministry, he went into Arabia and, "after three years he went up to Jerusalem to see Peter." Paul knew that Peter was an intimate of Jesus, and anxious to get first-hand information concerning His earthly life, His wonderful works, His awful death, and glorious resurrection, Paul commenced a casual interrogation of his new friend and brother.

"Tell me, Peter, where and when, and how, did you first become a Christian?"

"Well, it happened in this way. John the Baptist was baptizing and preaching in Bethabara, beyond Jordan. As he talked about Jesus, lo and behold, Jesus came along. When John saw Him he said, 'Behold the Lamb of God, which taketh away the sin of the world.' Among those who heard John and saw Jesus was my brother Andrew. One day he said to me, 'We have found the Messiah, which is, being interpreted, the Christ.' Nothing would do but that I go with him to where Jesus was. When Jesus saw me He said, 'Thou art Simon the son of Jona: thou shalt be called Cephas, which is by interpretation, A stone.'

Praise God, I became so enamored of my Savior that I left my boat and my nets and for three years, with Him and ten others, and a rascal by the name of Iscariot, we sailed the sea, tramped the roads, and climbed the hills."

"Tell me, Peter, *whose son do you think Jesus really was?*"

"What do you mean, Paul?"

"Well, just this. Already I have heard that Joseph, the carpenter, was His father, and although I know better, I would be so happy to hear from your lips a confirmation of my personal conviction."

In less time than I take to tell it, Peter started in, for when Peter got a chance to exalt Christ he needed no coaxing.

"One day, Paul, on the coast of Caesarea Phillippi, Jesus gathered us together, and after inquiring from the rest of the disciples what people said about Him, He looked me straight in the eyes and said, 'Whom do you say that I, the Son of Man, am?' Do you know, Paul, until that moment I was a little hazy concerning His Sonship, but when I opened my mouth to answer I seemed possessed of a supernatural wisdom, and I replied, 'Thou art the Christ, the Son of the Living God.' To my utter amazement He said, 'Blessed art thou, Simon Bar-Jona, flesh and blood hath not revealed it unto you, but my Father in heaven.'"

Isn't it wonderful, dear friends, to have such a revelation, through which our natural and national prejudices are broken down? It matters not to me whether you are Irish, English, or Scotch, a German, a Hollander, or a Swede, Chinese, African-American, or native American, if you have discovered that Jesus is the Son of the living God, let me shake your hand, for we are brothers. Hallelujah!

Before they lay down that night, Paul recited to Peter the story of his apprehension by Christ on the Damascus Road, his conversion, and his call to the ministry. As Peter listened with open mouth and moistened eyes to the triumph of the Gospel in a murderer's life, Paul waxed eloquent in the rehearsal of the details beginning from the moment when at noon he was stricken to the ground and blinded, until in a house "on the street called Straight" he prayed his first real prayer and received his marching orders from his God.

A Visit to Gethsemane and Calvary

Next morning ere the sun had risen, the two sinners, saved by grace, were out of bed. A simple meal was prepared and quietly eaten, for both men were thinking more than they were talking.

"Where would you like to go first, Paul? I could escort you through the temples and other places of beauty and interest around Jerusalem, but it is just as you say, I am your host, you are my guest, command me."

"If the choice is proffered to me, Peter, I would like to visit the battlefield upon which our blessed Redeemer, single-handed and alone, conquered sin and death and hell for us."

So across the brook Kidron into Gethsemane's garden they went. Upon a little knoll they sat down and for a few moments not a word was uttered. With trembling voice, at last Peter began:

"Oh, Paul, what a night, shall I ever forget it! Right over there amidst those olive trees He kneeled in prayer. He asked us to pray also, but we fell asleep. Grieved, no doubt, by our lethargy, He visited us three times reminding us of our responsibility, saying in His own sweet, gentle way, 'Could ye not watch with me one hour?' Then with a look of pity in His eye, He said, 'Sleep on now, and take your rest.' Never before nor since have I witnessed such agony of spirit as we beheld that night when Jesus prayed in this very garden. 'His sweat was as it were great drops of blood falling down to the ground.' Not long afterward we saw the lanterns, and the procession led by Judas, and you know the rest. For thirty pieces of silver Judas had sold his Christ, and betrayed Him into wicked hands."

Peter and Paul left the garden and the next thing we know *they are standing with bared heads upon the hill called Calvary.*

"I don't mind telling you, Peter," said Paul, "that among my chief reasons for visiting you was a desire to hear from you the truth about the dying day of God's Son."

"Oh, Paul, I hate to think of it. You have heard, no doubt, how I denied Him in Pilate's hall the night before. A little Roman servant girl sneered me right out of my religion, for with an oath I repudiated my allegiance to Him. I never saw Him again until with the holy women, I beheld Him walking up the hill bearing His cross. Beneath the burden He fell, and we sobbed in unison, 'My God, He is dead!' But no, He arose, yet so weakened in body that another, named Simon of Cyrene, had to carry His cross the rest of the way. We actually saw the brutal soldiers lay Him upon His back and drive the nails into His hands and feet. And do you know, Paul, when that cross was uplifted and planted in the ground, I think even yet I hear the tearing of His muscles. As with pitying eyes He beheld His bloody assassins, He said, 'Father, forgive them, for they know not what they do.'"

By this time Peter's voice so trembled that he could not go on. There on that place where Jesus suffered, bled, and died, Paul the murderer and Peter the fisherman wept together.

> O Jesus, Lord, how can it be,
> That Thou shouldst give Thy life for me?
> To bear the cross and agony,
> In that dread hour on Calvary!
> O Calvary! dark Calvary!
> Where Jesus shed His blood for me;
> O Calvary! blest Calvary!
> 'Twas there my Savior died for me.

Peter, resuming his description of that fearful event, said, "From the sixth hour until the ninth the heavens were darkened, and right there from that spot where you now stand I heard Him cry, 'My God, my God, why hast thou forsaken me?' The crowd responded with sneers while one of them took a sponge filled with vinegar and gave Him to drink. Weaker and weaker He grew, until at last He cried with a loud voice, 'Father, into thy hands I commend my spirit,' and He gave up the spirit."

As Paul wiped the tears from his eyes he said, "Peter, what is your particular theory of the Atonement?"

"Why, bless your heart, Paul, I never heard of such a thing."

"Well, the modernists say that just as a soldier dies on the battlefield for his country, and a mother suffers and dies giving birth to a child, so Christ died for the world."

"Blasphemy!" shouted Peter. "The death of our Redeemer must never be compared with the sacrificial death of any other before or since. 'Christ died, the just for the unjust, to bring us to God.' He tasted the misery of ten thousand hells in order that we poor sinners might escape the agony of one."

To this Paul replied, "What do you think of the martyr theory? That is, He merely sealed with His blood the principles He preached with His lips. Like every reformer, whether political or religious, He laid down His life for the cause He loved."

By this time Peter's eyes were flashing indignation and taking Paul by the lapel of the coat, he said, "Brother, if you and I are going to be successful ministers of the Gospel, we had better forget all this theory business and stick to the one sublime fact that Christ died for the ungodly. His death was no accident—He was born to bleed. Although He was crucified by wicked hands, He was slain by the 'determinate counsel and foreknowledge of God.'"

"God bless you, Peter, with you I agree, and in His strength, and by His help we shall tell poor guilty sinners the truth and nothing but the truth concerning the Cross."

So, down from Golgotha's hill they went, back to Peter's house, and after a season of prayer in which they thanked God for the atoning work of Christ, they retired for the night to sleep the "sleep of the just."

Their Meditation at the Tomb

The next place of sacred interest visited by Peter and Paul was Joseph of Arimathaea's tomb, not two angels in white apparel, but two sinners saved by grace, and rejoicing in the living Christ. There was the stone, but rolled away, and upon it our friends sat down. Paul broke the silence with a question.

"Tell me, Peter, do you believe that Jesus Christ arose from the dead? I am not talking about His Spirit. I refer to His corporeal resurrection. Did He or did He not rise in a body? Now don't look so bewildered until I have explained the reason for my apparent infidelity. The clever religious peddlers of pleasant platitudes are telling folks that Jesus is alive, and the gullible public think that these humanists are supernaturalists. I interrogated one of them the other day, and the way I caught him was by asking, 'Do you believe that on the morning of the third day Joseph's tomb was empty?' Then the rascal began to squirm and confess that the resurrection to him meant the survival of personality divorced from a body interred."

"Oh, pshaw, Paul! You didn't fall for that humbug, did you?"

"Glory to God, I didn't, Peter. I have come to you for first-hand information concerning the Resurrection. I hope to write an article about it some day and when I do, believe me, I shall make no apology for my faith in the living Lord."

"Well," said Peter, "I saw the empty tomb, I entered the place where He lay, and saw the grave clothes as He had neatly folded them away. On the morning of the third day, in the darkness of the sepulcher, He awakened, lit the lamp of immortality and walked out, and the lamp has been burning ever since."

> Death could not keep his prey,
> Jesus, my Savior!
> He tore the bars away,
> Jesus, my Lord!
>
> Up from the grave He arose,
> With a mighty triumph o'er His foes;
> He arose a victor from the dark domain,
> And He lives for ever with His saints to reign;
> He arose! He arose!
> Hallelujah! Christ arose!
>
> —Robert Lowry

"Why, Peter, how true it is if Christ be not risen our preaching is vain, and our faith is vain. Yes, and we are found false witnesses of God because we testified of God that He raised up Christ whom He raised not up. If so be that the modernists are right."

Oh, friends, how we ought to thank God for the faith that Peter and Paul possessed in the resurrection of our Lord. How wonderful to think that we are worshiping not a dead, historic Jesus, but a living, scriptural Christ. We may disagree on many minor details concerning our religious beliefs, but if we agree that Christ not only rose from the dead, but is alive forevermore, we can have sweet friendship.

A Day on the Mount

Before the fortnight's vacation was ended, at Paul's behest, Peter accompanied him to the hill from whence Christ went to heaven. One bonnie morning, while the sunbeams were playing amidst the pinnacles of the temple, and the birds were making melody in their hearts, our two friends were standing with bared heads upon Mount Olivet, the one anxious to hear the truth about the ascension, and the other eager to talk. Peter began while Paul listened.

"It was upon this mount, Brother Paul, (by this time they were calling each other brother) that we received from the resurrected Christ our marching orders. He didn't tell us to go and clean up the world by social service, nor dry up breweries by legislation; He gave us no commission to build hospitals and schools, nor to make the world safe for democracy."

At this juncture Paul interrupted Peter—

"Just a minute, Peter, aren't you in sympathy with social service, education, and the alleviation of human suffering?"

"Most certainly I am, Paul, and wherever the Gospel is preached, and the Word of God permitted to hold sway, you may be sure that these blessings will follow as by-products of salvation. Christ said to us, 'Go ye into all the world and preach the Gospel to every creature, baptizing them in the name of the Father, and of the Son, and of the Holy Spirit: teaching them to observe all things whatsoever I have commanded you: and lo, I am with you alway, even unto the end of the age.'"

"In other words," said Paul, "instead of installing hot and cold water, shower baths, tiled floors and electric lights in the pig pen, our business is to deliver the prodigal from the fellowship of the swine and bring him to his Father's house."

"Precisely, Paul. I am so glad that you are straight on the great commission, for some of these fellows in Jerusalem are preaching politics and reformation, and already quite a few have exhausted the Bible and are now reviewing books on a Sunday night—they make me sick. Let you and me stick to the proclamation of the blessed old Gospel.

"I have digressed a little from what I was originally telling you, so I must get back to my story. While we were listening to Him give us our instruction, lo, He began to go up. None of us had ever witnessed the like before, and you can imagine with what consternation and bewilderment we beheld the unique spectacle."

"Honestly, Peter did you actually see Him ascend?"

"Why Paul, until He vanished from our view we saw the print of the nails in the soles of His feet, and then a cloud received Him out of our sight, and we saw Him no more. While we looked steadily toward heaven as He went up, behold, two men stood by us in white apparel who also said, 'Ye men of Galilee, why stand ye gazing up into heaven? this same Jesus, which is taken up from you into heaven, shall so come in like manner as ye have seen him go into heaven.'"

"Say, Paul, do you believe that Jesus is coming again?"

"Most certainly I do, Peter, and apart from that wonderful event we have no blessed hope. We might well sigh in vain for the touch of a vanished hand, or the sound of a voice that is still. We will never fellowship with our departed dead again if Christ does not return. Some even now are saying that every time a dear old lady with a philanthropic heart gives a bag of potatoes or a shoulder of beef to a poor family, that Jesus has come again. Others teach that when we die, that is His return."

"Och, it is too silly to even refute, Paul. The angel told us that we shall see Him come in like manner as we saw Him go. What do we care for the carnal reasoning of benighted minds? If every man and woman on the face of God's earth disbelieved in the Lord's return I tell you, Paul, I'll continue to embrace what the angel told us on that memorable day upon this mount."

I can almost hear the "amens," and "hallelujahs" of these two redeemed sinners as they exulted in the blessed hope of the church. My friends, do you believe that Jesus is coming again? Never mind if your ignorance concerning the details of His advent has banished you to the wilderness of eschatological loneliness, so long as you know that Christ is coming again, God bless you, I am with you, shake my hand.

> Jesus is coming! His saints to release,
> Coming to give to the warring earth peace;
> Sinning and sighing, and sorrow shall cease,
> Jesus is coming again!

What enabled those two apparent opposites to enjoy each other's company for two weeks? They believed in the deity of Christ, His blood atonement for sinners, His bodily resurrection, His ascension, and His coming again. Do you?

The Last Day of the Vacation

After fourteen blessed days of fellowship together, Peter and Paul anticipated the morning of the fifteenth with mixed feelings, happy because they had met, and sad because they must part.

"Before I go, Peter, I would like to stand just once more on the spot where I stood the day Stephen was stoned to death."

"But Paul, why resurrect the past? Your sins, like mine, are under the blood, buried in the sea of God's forgiveness to be remembered no more against us."

"I am well aware of that, brother, but inasmuch as I purpose preaching the Gospel to people who now are as I once was, permit me to go back and allow the memory of that bloody day to remind me of the pit from whence I have been digged."

Together they stood at the historic place where the first martyr sealed his testimony with his blood. With glassy eye, and trembling voice, Paul rehearsed the pathetic details, especially his part in the crime.

"Ah, Peter, I am convinced that the first link in the chain of circumstances leading to my conversion was the homegoing of Stephen. I hated the Christians, I despised the Nazarene, and agreed with the chief priest and other members of the synagogue that this man was a blasphemer. But do you know, as I listened to that marvelous message he delivered, it soon became apparent that he had something my religion had never produced in me. Afterward I learned that he was filled with the Spirit. My, didn't he handle that Old Testament like an expert! And when he concluded his message he shook his fist in our faces and said, 'Ye stiffnecked and uncircumcised in heart and ears, ye do always resist the Holy Spirit: as your fathers did, so do ye.' When they heard these things they were cut to the heart, and they gnashed on him with their teeth.

"The wilder they grew the calmer he became, and looking up into heaven he said, 'Behold, I see the Son of man standing on the right hand of God.' That was enough. They stopped their ears and rushed upon him, cast him out of the city and stoned him to death."

"But Paul," said Peter, "did you throw any of the missiles?"

"No, Peter, but I held the coats of the rascals who did, therefore, I was just as guilty as they."

By this time Paul was sobbing as though his heart would break.

"Peter, when I get to heaven, I want to see my Savior first of all, and then Stephen. Although I went on breathing out slaughter against the Christians, the memory of Stephen's death could never be erased from my mind, and reacted upon me as an arrow in the side of a wounded stag. Just before he died, he said, 'Lord Jesus, receive my spirit,' and he kneeled down and cried with a loud voice,

'Lord, lay not this sin to their charge.' And when he had said this, he fell asleep.

"Tomorrow you and I shall part company, Peter, maybe never more to meet on earth. Before we go shall we kneel on the spot where I contributed to that deacon's death, and promise God that by His grace we shall live as Stephen lived, preach as he preached, and if need be, die as he died."

Ah, dear friends, we have been visiting the historic arena of the world's redemption, we have been reminded of our past wicked lives. But just as Paul and Peter were forgiven, so are we. Their Christ is ours, and even though we may never be crucified upside down as was Peter, or decapitated as was Paul, for Jesus sake, let us have no desire to

> . . . be carried to the skies
> On flowery beds of ease,
> While others fought to win the prize
> And sailed through bloody seas.
> —Isaac Watts

The parting on the fifteenth day was sacred, for I am sure those two great men not only shook hands, but kissed each other good-bye. Peter stood at the door of his little house meditating upon the memory of these blessed days. He watched Saul of Tarsus, with a bundle over his shoulders, disappear around the bend of the road. I think I hear him say, "Thank God for the Gospel that can save a man like that, for grace that is greater than all our sin."

NOTES

The Effect of Pentecost upon Peter

Joseph Parker (1830–1902) was one of England's most popular preachers. Largely self-educated, Parker had pulpit gifts that soon moved him into leadership among the Congregationalists. He was a fearless and imaginative preacher who attracted both common people and the aristocracy, and he was particularly a "man's preacher." His *People's Bible* is a collection of the shorthand reports of the sermons and prayers Parker delivered as he preached through the entire Bible in seven years (1884–91). He pastored the Poultry Church, London, later called the City Temple, from 1869 until his death.

This sermon is taken from Volume 22 of *The People's Bible* (London: Hazell, Watson and Viney, 1900).

Joseph Parker

2

THE EFFECT OF PENTECOST UPON PETER

Acts 2:22–36

THIS IS A FULL LENGTH portrait of Peter himself. If we see clearly the effect upon Peter, we shall have a true idea of the effect of the outpouring of the Holy Spirit upon the entire church. God shows us things that are too great to be seen in their completeness, in illustrative and easily-comprehended parts. Those who carefully study Peter's speech in answer to the mockers will see in the case of one man the effect which would follow by the loving acceptance of the inspiration of the Spirit on the part of the whole church. Inspiration is followed by self-revelation; a man may thus reveal himself with perfect unconsciousness. Peter is not an egotist in this case, but, so to say, the passive instrument through which the Holy Spirit delivers new and gracious messages to the church. Fix your minds therefore upon Peter in the first instance. We know what he has been up to this time—ardent, impulsive, unbalanced, enthusiastic, cowardly. Since we last saw him, during the days of the bodily-present Christ, he has been the subject of Pentecostal influence. We have therefore to look on this picture and on that, and upon the change discoverable between the two pictures you may found your estimate of the value of spiritual inspiration.

Heroic Eloquence

Notice his heroic eloquence. He is not only a speaker, he is a burning speaker It is not enough to speak—you may teach an automaton to speak, you may so instruct a machine as to utter a mimic cry. This man is not only speaking words, he is speaking them with unction, with fire, with emphasis never heard in his tone before. A man

23

does not read simply because he pronounces words that are in the text that he is perusing, a man does not give out a psalm simply because he articulates without inaccuracy every individual word in the meter. There is something in the reading which cannot be put into type, a halo, or say an atmosphere, or say an aroma, or say an illustrative and far-reaching fire of the soul.

It is even so with this speech of Peter. You have not the whole speech in the words. You must be enabled, by a kind of semi-inspiration of your own, to read between the lines in order to get hold of all the force and weight of this burning oration. We do not gather all from the speaker that we gather when we take down the mere words which he utters: there are palpitations which cannot be reported, and tones which have no typal representation. It was emphatically so in this great speech of the inspired fisherman. It carries everything before it like a fire marching through dry stubble. Already therefore in the mere matter of eloquence, we discover a wonderful change in the man who denied his Lord with an oath. He was always an ardent man, but now he burns as he says the elements themselves will one day "burn with fervent heat." Who but he himself could have put those two words together? They are part of his very self. Others might have said, "The elements will burn"; they might even have gone so far as to say "the elements will burn with heat," but it was Peter's very self that said, "the elements shall burn with fervent heat." That fervent heat, in its own degree and with its own proper spiritual limits, we find in this great deliverance.

Profound Insight into Scripture

It was not only eloquence, it was reasoning on fire. For notice Peter's grasp of biblical truth. Who had ever known Peter before as a reader—who was aware until this moment that Peter ever opened the sacred Book and perused it with a student's curiosity and eagerness? We had never thought of Peter as an expositor; an errand-runner, a zealous, not always well-balanced friend, a crude thinker, an incoherent speaker—under these terms we may have formed some conception of the apostolic fisherman, but certainly it never entered into our minds that he had been a reader, a student, an inquirer into the deep decrees and hidden things of the sanctuary—yet in a moment he opens the prophecy of Joel, and reads it in the language and tone of his own day, and then he searches into some of the richest psalms of David, and quotes from them enough to establish the continuity and solidity of his great argument.

Not only was he transformed into an orator, he was transformed into a profound expositor of the divine purpose in the creation and education of the church. He speaks like a philosopher. He sees that the ages are not unrelated days, broken and incohesive nights, but that the ages are one, as the day is one, from its gray dawn to the time of the lighting of the evening star. This always follows deep acquaintance with the mysteries of God and high fellowship with the Spirit of the living One. We are delivered from the vexation and torment of daily details, and are set in the great currents and movements of the divine purpose, and thereby do we acquire the balance which gives us rest and serenity, which often glows into courageous joy. Think of Peter, a fisherman, uniting these, and calling upon prophecy as its own witness, and pointing out how life is a development, a growing upward and onward, and outward, into new and harmonious expressions. When the church is inspired, it will be eloquent; when the church is inspired it will be biblically wise, it will be able to read not the letter only, but to decipher the spirit, and to read the letter so that it will quiver into music under the tone refined in the sanctuary and made alive with the vitality of God.

Strong Grasp of the Meaning and Purpose of Prophecy

Peter shows us how prophecy is fulfilled. The fulfillment of prophecy is not something which God has been arduously trying to do and has at last barely accomplished. The fulfillment of prophecy is not a divine effort; God is not a great giant trying to carry some infinite globe up an infinite hill, and at last just succeeding in unloading the burden. The fulfillment of prophecy is a natural process, and it comes to express a natural end. Prophecy is not to

God a mere hope, it is a clear vision of what must be, and of what He Himself will bring to pass. You do not prophesy that the child will become a man; you speak of his manhood as future, but quite certain; you say what he will be, strong, wise, chivalrous, gentle, prudent, brave—and in so saying you are not expressing the result of an arduous effort on your part which you hope to bring to a successful issue, but you are taking your stand by the side of God when He created the typal Adam, and you say this is God's purpose and Adam shall come to this estate.

We want the right way of reading the fulfillment of prophecy. It is prophesied that the whole earth shall be filled with the knowledge of the Lord. It is not a mere hope, it is the sure outcome of the divine way of doing things. Christ must, by a necessity which cannot be explained, even by the necessity of righteousness and light and truth, reign until He has put all enemies under His feet. So we are not trusting to a vain promise; prophecy is not a daring expression of a fanatical hope, it is God's prevision of the future, and God's note of hand that He will yet give His Son the heathen for an inheritance, and the uttermost parts of the earth for a possession, signed in every ink in the universe, signed in heaven before the earth was formed, signed on Calvary with the blood-ink of the Cross. We must rest in this assurance; the Word of the Lord will prevail, not by means of education, eloquence, or mechanical efforts on the part of the church, but the world will be converted to Christ because God has said it will be so, and when His Word has gone forth it cannot return to Him void.

Powerful Apologist of Doctrine and Truth

Not only was Peter eloquent and instructive—he startled the church by becoming its most solid and convincing reasoner. What a wonderful argument this is, to take no higher view of it in the meantime. "Ye men of Israel," said Peter, "hear these words," and mark how cunning the words are, in the best sense of the term. Observe where and how Peter begins his address. "Jesus of Nazareth, a *Man*," there is no appeal to theological bias or prejudice.

Had he begun by saying to such people, "Jesus of Nazareth, the incarnate God," he would have lost his audience in his first sentence. He was made into a master of assemblies, he began where his hearers could begin, and he who begins otherwise than at the point of sympathy, however eloquent, will lose the reins ere he has time to put one sentence to another. Already therefore this inspiration is beginning to tell in the mental force and astuteness of this unlettered fisherman. He gives up the deity of Christ, does he? He plainly calls Jesus Christ "a man approved of God among you by miracles and wonders and signs which God did by him in the midst of you, as ye yourselves also know." But does he conclude so? He begins by describing Christ as a Man, but the glittering point of his glorious climax is this—"Therefore let all the house of Israel know assuredly, that God hath made that same Jesus, whom ye have crucified, both Lord and Christ."

Note the argumentative skill. Had Peter broken off his speech in the first sentence, the coldest Socinian that ever wrote about Christ could have endorsed his utterance, but Peter makes way through scriptural quotations and through inspired exposition, until he concludes with this burning breath, "God hath made that same Jesus, whom ye have crucified, both Lord and Christ."

Notice, too, how Peter stands without equivocation upon the historical fact of the Resurrection. He was not talking to people who lived a century after the reported rising again of Christ: he was talking to those who knew perfectly well what had happened. Does he put any gloss upon the matter—does he seek to make it a parable, a typal instance, a quasi resurrection? He talks with the absolute frankness of a man who is relating facts, which every child in the assembly knew to be such, and he was in the presence of people who could instantly have risen and contradicted the statements which he made, had they been in a position to do so.

Does Peter separate Christ from the wonderful manifestation of the Spirit which had been granted? On the contrary, he connects Pentecost with the risen and glorified Son of God. This enables him to use another "therefore." I refer to these therefores in this connection because we are trying to show how inspiredly argumentative the apostle had become. "Therefore being by the right hand of God exalted, and having received of the Father the promise of the Holy Spirit, he hath shed forth this, which ye now see and hear." *This* is His last miracle, *this* is the spiritualization of all the miracles, this is the marvel to which all signs and wonders were leading up, this is the capital without which the column would have been unfinished, this the revelation of the purpose which moved His heart when he came to save the world and found His church.

It was also a great evangelical speech which Peter made. He gave the house of Israel a new chance. "Therefore let all the house of Israel know assuredly"—it is as if Peter would say, "Now you have the opportunity of escaping all the past and beginning a new and glorious future." That is the continual speech of Christianity. Every morning Christianity says, "You can make today better than yesterday. Every morning is a new chance, every new year is a new opportunity, every turn in the affairs of humanity is a new gate opened upon some higher road." Would that we had understanding of these things and could turn our chances to high spiritual use!

A Standard for the Church

All these features will characterize a revived church. We shall have heroic eloquence, profound insight into Scripture, strong grasp of the meaning and purpose of prophecy, and we shall ourselves become unanswerably argumentative in all Christian doctrine and truth when the Holy Spirit is poured out upon us.

We have in Peter a standard whereby to measure ourselves. When the Holy Spirit falls upon us we shall go to the Bible with a new reading power, and we shall see wonders where before we saw nothing because of our spiritual blindness. There are portions of the Bible with which we are nominally familiar, but what do we know of its inner meanings, of the minor prophets, the out-of-the-way histories, the deep things of God? Under the enlightenment of the Spirit we shall see that everything grand in thought, thrilling in poetry, tragic in experience, noble in heroism, is in the Bible. This is the Book out of which all other books are made. All science is here, all history all fiction, all philosophy, all poetry, even the best titles of all books are in the Bible. There is nothing in any literature whose root is not to be found in the inspired volume. This is the Book out of which all other books are made, as the earth is the quarry out of which all its palaces have been dug, and as there are grander palaces in the rocks and woods than have yet been built, so there are more glorious visions in the Bible than we have yet beheld.

How slowly we realize that everything that is upon the earth actually came out of the earth itself. Is the marble palace superb? It was dug out of the earth. Is the city vast and noble—the glittering Jerusalem, imperial Rome, immeasurable Babylon and Nineveh? They were all dug out of the heart of the earth. Is the navy proud and strong? It was all cut out of the forests which fed themselves at the breast of mother earth. There is nothing upon the earth which did not come out of the earth itself. It is even so with this Bible. You have a thousand libraries, but they all came out of God's Book, yes, the libraries that were founded, if any such there were ages before the Book was written, came out of the Book. God is older than any book that can be written: inspiration is the most ancient fact in all history, yes, it antedates all history and makes all history possible. There are those who want to run away from the Bible and set up other books, as though they were independent and original. I will believe in their independence and originality as soon as you show me one block of polished marble that did not come out of the earth. Prove to me that you stole it from some of the upper stars, then I will believe in the independence and originality of the marble block. My own deep conviction is that the time will come when every other book will fling itself, so to say, in loyal homage at the foot of God's Book and say, "Whatever is good in me I owe to you." The earth grows no polished marble: the old earth will polish no blocks for you; she will, so to say, grow them for you, hold them in custody until you come for them with great iron keys and open the recesses within which she preserves them. Polishing you will have to do, squaring and measuring, all this you will have to do, but the solid block itself came out of the heart of the earth. So with all books that are good and true and wise and useful; they have their vital relation to God's Book, in whatever language written, in whatever country published, though in those languages and in those countries the Book we call God's has not yet been known.

Why do men limit inspiration—why do men want to yet trace any good thing to any source but God? If there is anything good in Mahommedanism, I claim it for Christ: He was before all things. If there is anything good in Brahmanism, I claim it for Christ. If there is anything good in the heart of the wildest savage that this day tears his fellow creatures in lands of barbarism, I claim it for Christ. My Christ is more than a merely historical figure, born on a certain day, and on a certain day crucified: the Christ in whom I believe is always born, always crucified—the same yesterday, today, and forever, not a name upon a calendar, but a name that hides itself under the foundations of everything solid, above everything brilliant, and around everything wide, and that crowns with everlasting glory everything philanthropic and noble.

As the earth owes nothing to any other world but her light, so God has made people that we carry everything in us but our own inspiration. He does not make us new in the sense of losing our old identity; He makes us new by His inspiration in the sense of lifting us up to the full expression of His own holy purpose in our original creation. We cannot inspire ourselves. The Holy Spirit is the gift of God. We are made in the divine image and likeness, we have wondrous faculties as the earth has wondrous treasures—all these are the gift of God, all these we hold in stewardship for God. But these will be in us so many weights and burdens, curses rather than blessings, unless there falls upon us the mighty Pentecostal Holy Spirit. Then shall we be our true selves, eloquent, wise, argumentative, strong, evangelical, sympathetic, new creatures in Christ Jesus through whom the Holy Spirit has been shed abroad in our hearts.

NOTES

Peter

John Daniel Jones (1865–1942) served for forty years at the Richmond Hill Congregational Church in Bournemouth, England, where he ministered the Word with a remarkable consistency of quality and effectiveness, as his many volumes of published sermons attest. A leader in his denomination, he gave himself to church extension (he helped to start thirty new churches), assistance to needier congregations, and increased salaries for the clergy. He spoke at D. L. Moody's Northfield Conference in 1919.

This sermon is from his book, *The Glorious Company of the Apostles*, published by James Clarke and Co., London.

J. D. Jones

3

PETER

And when Jesus beheld him, he said, Thou art Simon the son of Jona: thou shalt be called Cephas, which is by interpretation, A stone [Peter] (John 1:42).

THERE ARE TO BE FOUND in the Gospels three separate and distinct lists of the twelve apostles, and an examination of those lists reveals the fact that there are variations in the order in which the names of the apostles are mentioned. The holy Evangelists are not agreed as to which of the apostles should be mentioned second, which third, which fourth, which seventh, which eighth, which tenth, and which eleventh. But however much they may differ as to intermediate names, they are absolutely agreed as to which name should be first and which name should be last. At the end of Matthew's list and Mark's list and Luke's list you will find the name of Judas—"who also betrayed Him." At the head of Matthew's list and Mark's list and Luke's list you will find the name of Simon the son of John, who also was surnamed Peter. The place of shame and ignominy and eternal dishonor belongs by universal consent to the traitor; and by an equally clear and indisputable title the place of leadership and primacy belongs to Simon Peter.

Now, it is by no accident or mere chance that the name of Simon Peter in every case heads the list of the holy and blessed Twelve. Peter's name comes first because, without controversy or dispute, he was the natural prince and leader of the apostolic company. We may repudiate, and we *do* repudiate, the preposterous claims made for Peter by the Roman Church, for the simple reason that they have no shred of support in history or fact. Jesus Christ conferred no spiritual privilege or prerogative on Peter which He did not also bestow upon his associates in the

33

apostolic college. Rome bases the stupendous claims it makes for Peter upon the supposition that certain unique powers were conferred upon him by Christ after he had made the great confession. But in other parts of the New Testament I find the very same power conferred upon the other apostles. "Upon this rock," said Christ to Peter on that great day in the apostle's history, "will I build My church." But when I turn to the Book of Revelation, I find that it is not upon Peter alone that the church is built, but the city has twelve foundations, and upon those foundations the names of the twelve apostles of the Lamb. "Whatsoever thou shalt bind on earth shall be bound in heaven, and whatsoever thou shalt loose on earth shall be loosed in heaven," said Christ to Peter on that same supreme never-to-be-forgotten occasion. But I pass on from the sixteenth to the eighteenth of Matthew, and I find Christ, in precisely identical terms, conferring that same wonderful and mysterious prerogative upon all the Twelve. No! Christ conferred no special or unique powers upon Peter. He bestowed upon him no lordship or authority over his brethren. For the Catholic theory of an official primacy there is not the slightest shadow of foundation. But while thus repudiating that claim, I for one frankly and unreservedly admit that Peter did exercise a kind of primacy among the Twelve. But the primacy he exercised was not the primacy of office, but the primacy of character. Gather any twelve people together, and before they have been in company a week the one of strongest character among them—though unadorned by any trappings of office, and bearing no title of rank or dignity—will inevitably assert himself as leader, and exercise supremacy over the rest. Now Simon Peter was by nature a strong, masterful man. He had a certain force and energy of character that fitted him, and inevitably made him a leader of men. Had we but Peter's early history written out for us, I am persuaded we would find that he had been a leader among the fishermen of the lake and a leader among the townspeople of Bethsaida before he became the prince and leader of the Twelve. Indeed, Peter was the kind of man who would be prominent anywhere, and the very same qualities that made him prominent in the town of Bethsaida and the fishing circles of Galilee speedily put him in the first place in this glorious company of the apostles.

That Peter was first among the Twelve—*primus inter pares*—the prince and leader of the Twelve, no one with the New Testament before him can for a moment doubt. For the Gospels are full of Peter. Yes, next to our Lord, it is Peter of whom the Gospels most often speak. Of some of the apostles we know absolutely nothing but their names—preserved for us in the Evangelists' lists. And even of the greatest of the glorious company—James and John and Andrew—the pictures given to us in the Gospels are dim and vague and shadowy; but the picture of Peter is detailed and vivid and lifelike. And that is how we always see Peter—as the leader of the Twelve. He asks questions for the Twelve; he makes suggestions for the Twelve; he expresses opinions in the name of the Twelve. The official primacy of the Roman Catholic Church we repudiate, but the fact that Peter exercised a primacy among the twelve, springing from his own bold, masterful, and impetuous nature, is a fact written large upon every page of the New Testament.

The Contrasts in Peter's Nature

Now, when I read certain passages in the Gospels, I do not wonder that Peter was acknowledged, without cavil or dispute, as the prince and leader of the Twelve, even though a saintly and seraphic John was of the company. For at times Peter is an inspired man, and scales the heavens. He has his moments of rapture and high vision when he is fit to take his place by the side of Moses and David and Isaiah. When the disciples found that miraculous draught of fishes enclosed within their nets, it was only on Peter's soul that there flashed a new sense of the holiness and majesty of Christ, and of the whole apostolic company he was the only one to fall at Christ's feet and cry, "Depart from me, for I am a sinful man, O Lord." When after those hard sayings in Capernaum the crowds were deserting Jesus Christ, and He turned to His disciples with the pathetic, heart-breaking question, "Will ye also go away," it was to Peter's generous and loving soul that there came the great and immortal answer, "Lord, to whom shall we go? Thou hast the words of eternal life." And when again, in Caesarea, Christ made that wistful inquiry, "Whom say ye that I am?" It was the inspired Peter who made that high reply, "Thou art the Christ, the Son of the living God." Yes, when I read of the incident on the lake, and the answer in Capernaum, and the confession in Caesarea, I do not wonder that the first place among the Twelve was given to a man of such insight and vision and rapture as this.

But there are other passages in the Gospels which, when I read, I marvel that Peter was among the Twelve at all. When I come across those passages in which Peter begins to boast, I marvel that he was among the Twelve at all. When I read of his presuming to correct and rebuke the Christ, I marvel that he was among the Twelve at all. When I read about his sleeping in the garden, I marvel that he was among the Twelve at all. And when I read of that terrible and shameful episode in the judgment hall, I marvel that instead of coming down to us as the prince and chief of the apostles, Peter, the denier and the blasphemer, did not make his bed with Judas the betrayer in the lowest hell.

There are violent and extreme contrasts in the character of Peter. None of the apostles soared to such heights as he, and none, save the son of perdition, sank to such awful depths. None heard such words of praise from the lips of Christ, and none such terrible words of reproach. Cast your eye over his history. One day you find him winning from Christ the most magnificent eulogy His lips ever pronounced. "Blessed art thou, Simon Bar Jona, for flesh and blood hath not revealed it unto thee, but my Father, which is in heaven." On another you find him provoking from the Lord that most scathing of rebukes, "Get thee behind me, Satan, thou art a stumbling block unto me." At one time you find him the companion of the Savior on the blessed Mount, on another you find him cursing and swearing he did not know the Man. Yes, according to the Gospel Peter was both saint and grievous sinner. Like Paul, he was at times snatched up into the seventh heaven, and, like Dante, at other times he saw hell; one day you find him in the heavenly places in Christ Jesus, and another day you find him in the horrible pit. Indeed, so startling is the contrast that we could scarcely believe that the man of Caesarea and the blasphemer of the judgment hall were one and the same person, did we not carry the confirmation of it in our own bosoms. We have but to look within and we shall know this picture of Peter is drawn from life, for we shall see those same violent, amazingly and almost unbelievable contrasts in our own hearts.

Is it possible, you say, for one to behold the glory of the Lord on the mount and then to forsake Him in the garden? Is it possible for one to confess Christ in Caesarea, and then forswear Him in the judgment hall? Yes, it is quite possible. Look into your own hearts, and you will know it is quite possible. Gaze steadily and bravely into that awful abyss, your own heart, and you will know it is quite possible. For in your own heart you will see both heaven and hell, aspirations and desires born of God, and hideous lusts of foulnesses that issue from the pit. And with heaven and hell in these deceitful and desperately wicked hearts of ours we reproduce today Peter's history. Yes, I will be very bold to say we can parallel Peter's history by our own. We have known something—most of us, at any rate—of the bliss that filled Peter's soul upon the mount, and of the brave enthusiasm that fired his heart at Caesarea. Yes, we have had our days when we were fellow citizens of the saints and of the household of God. But if we have shared Peter's bliss, we have also shared his sin and shame. We have forsaken our Lord as he did, and we have denied Him before others as he did. Yes, there have been days in our experience when we have sinned so grievously and desperately as almost to be beyond forgiveness. The human heart is the best confirmation of Peter's history. Heaven and hell contended for the mastery in Peter's heart long ago; heaven and hell are contending for the mastery in our divided and distracted souls today.

The Evolution of Peter

"Thou art Simon, the son of John," said Jesus, when He first set eyes upon this man who was to become the chief of the apostles. "Thou art Simon, thou shalt be called Cephas," which is by interpretation Peter—that is, "a rock." And if I had to search the New Testament through I could not discover a more beautiful illustration of the charity and hopefulness of our blessed Lord than I find in these His first words to Peter. For when Simon came to Him that day he was anything but a "rock." He was a man of sand that day, and for many a day after that. It took months, it took years, it took a lifetime to turn Simon into Peter—to turn the man of sand into the man of rock.

"In a gallery in Europe," says Dr. Miller in his little book, *The Friendship of Jesus,* "there hang side by side Rembrandt's first picture, a simple sketch, imperfect and faulty, and his great masterpiece which all men admire. And so in the two names, Simon and Peter, we have first the rude fisherman, the man as He was before Jesus began His work on him, and, second, the man as he became after the friendship of Jesus and the teaching of Jesus and the discipline of life had wrought their transformations in him." "Thou shalt be called the Rock," said Jesus about this man when he was brought to Him at the first by Andrew his brother. With the love that hopes all things our Lord hoped and believed and prophesied that Simon would become a man of rock-like steadfastness, as unmoved by the wrath and spite of men as the black bastions that line our coasts are by the waves that fret and foam at their feet.

But for long it seemed as if Christ's prophecy and hope would be disappointed. For Simon in the Gospels is a weak and vacillating creature. It is the man of sand you see in the man who ran away in the garden and who denied Christ with oaths and curses in the judgment hall at the taunt of a serving maid. Yet Christ bated not a jot of heart or hope for His fallen disciple. "Thou shalt be called Peter," He said again to his penitent and well-nigh despairing soul, and in a few weeks you find that same

man who fled in the garden speaking boldly in the name
of the Lord Jesus in the streets of Jerusalem, and wit-
nessing courageously for Him before governors and kings.
Yes, he is the man of sand all through the gospels; but in
the book of the Acts, on the day of Pentecost, at the temple
gate called Beautiful, before the Sanhedrim—he is Peter
the Rock.

And yet I will not say that Simon never turned coward after Pentecost—that he was always a man of rock
after Pentecost. To the end of life he was always contending with the weakness and cowardice of his own
heart, and more than once he fell as he did in the judgment hall. Once in Antioch, for fear of some Jews from
Jerusalem, he withdrew like a craven and a poltroon
from the fellowship of the Gentile Christians, and so
stirred Paul's righteous soul to burning indignation and
provoked from him a public rebuke. And again, if the
legend be true, toward the end of his life he turned
coward at Rome. It was the time of the fierce and terrible Neronic persecutions. Christians were being put to
death in awful and unheard-of ways. And Peter's soul,
as he heard of Christians serving as lighted torches in
Nero's gardens, and dying hideous deaths in Roman
amphitheaters, clean fainted within him, and to escape
death he fled from Rome. But as he hurried along the
Appian Way, about two miles from the gates, he was
met by the Savior traveling toward the city. Struck with
amazement, Peter cried, *"Domine, quo vadis?"* ("Lord,
whither goest Thou?") And the Savior, looking upon him
as He had looked upon him long before in the judgment
hall, said, "I go to Rome to be crucified a second time." It
was Peter's last failure. It was the last trace of the sand
in his nature. He was Peter the Rock from that day to
the end. He returned to Rome, with head erect and proud
step, to witness bravely for Christ until such day as in
the barrack square he hung head downward on the cross
for his Lord's dear sake. And when I think of Peter's
history, of his many and shameful falls and his final
victory, two truths come home to my soul with mighty
power.

The Forgiving Grace of Christ

And this first I get from Simon Peter's history: a new and subduing idea of the forgiving grace of Christ. "Lord," Simon had said to Jesus one day, "how oft shall my brother sin against me and I forgive him? Till seven times?" Well was it for Simon that his thoughts on forgiveness were not his Master's. Had Jesus accepted Simon's notions about the limits of forgiveness Simon would never have reached the pearly gates, he would never have entered the inheritance of the saints in light, he would never have worn the crown and the robe of righteousness. Had Jesus adopted Simon's limits of forgiveness, then Simon himself would have been today in the outer darkness, where there is weeping and wailing and gnashing of teeth. "I say not unto thee until seven times," was our Lord's reply, "but until seventy times seven." And Simon needed the seventy times seven. For he sinned and sinned and sinned again. For he fell and fell and fell again. Simon himself is an illustration of grace that never wearies of forgiving. Yes, Simon is a monument of the patient and pardoning love of Christ. I have fancied that many a time and oft Peter used to say to his soul, anticipating the words of our own Gospel poet: "O to grace how great a debtor, daily I'm constrained to be." And again and again I am persuaded he used to take himself as a text and preach a sermon of comfort and hope to downcast and despairing souls. And when he came to die it was a saying of his beloved brother Paul that he wished to have graven on his tombstone, and that was this: "Where sin abounded, grace did much more abound." And with Peter as my text I would preach that same comforting sermon he used to preach long ago. Yes, I know we have sinned grievously and sinned often, but Jesus forgives even to seventy times seven. I say, even to seventy times seven. Friends may cast you off, parents may disown you, all who know you may despair of you, but there is mercy with Jesus Christ. Men and women laden with iniquities sinning and sinning and sinning again, I know of One who has not despaired of you; I know of One whose patience has not failed. Come to Peter's Savior, and you shall find that—

Unwearied in forgiveness still,
His heart can only love.

The Restoring Power of Christ

And this second thing I learn from Peter's story. I get a new idea of the restoring power of Christ. "Thou shalt be called Peter—a Rock," said Jesus. To turn Simon—the unstable, unreliable, vacillating Simon—into a rock! What a work was that! But the power of Christ accomplished it, so that the man who cursed at the taunt of a serving maid faced without a tremor a hideous death at Rome. And with Peter as my text I am prepared to preach this glorious Gospel this morning. There is not a person, however wicked and broken and helpless, that Jesus cannot by His Almighty power restore. "Thou shalt become a rock," Christ says to you and me—brave, strong, steadfast, immovable. To you, young man, frightened of your associates in the shop, Christ says, "Thou shalt become a rock," absolutely unshaken by their taunts or sneers or laughter. To you the victim of sin, hating it and doing it, loathing it and returning to it, and half inclined to abandon the struggle as hopeless, Christ says, "Thou shalt become a rock," against which temptation shall break in vain. To you of weak will and irresolute purpose, Christ says, "Thou shalt become a rock," steadfast, immovable, always abounding in the work of the Lord. Yet, with Peter as my text, I preach the restorability of the weakest and most despairing. The hand that made out of Simon a rock, the hand that made out of John and Mark a witness and a faithful martyr, the hand that made out of a drunken waif the greatest temperance worker of modern times can take us—weak, timid, broken as we are—and make us pillars in the temple of our God, from which we shall no more go out.

Peter's Pride

And now I have left myself but I moment or two to speak of Peter's chief fault and his chief virtue. His chief fault was his pride, his boastful and braggart self-confidence. I am not trying to utter a paradox, but simply

stating literal truth when I say that the very energy and
force and masterfulness of Peter's nature which consti-
tuted him the leader of the Twelve was also the direct
and immediate cause of his most bitter humiliations and
falls. The secret of victorious strength in the Christian life
is self-distrust. "When I am weak," so the apostle Paul
puts it in a sentence, "then am I strong." For when a man
realizes his weakness, he casts himself upon God, and
then he is able to overcome the principalities and powers
and spiritual hosts of wickedness which are drawn up to
do battle against his soul. Now that was a secret Peter
did not learn for many a day. There were certain words of
our Lord, such as, "Apart from Me ye can do nothing,"
which, as far as Peter was concerned, fell on absolutely
deaf ears. This strong, forceful, masterful man had complete and perfect confidence in himself. "Though all men
should be offended in Thee, I will never be offended."
"Simon, Simon," said our Lord to him in solemn warning,
"behold, Satan hath desired to have you, that he may sift
you as wheat, but I made supplication for thee, that thy
faith fail not quite." But Peter was hurt, almost insulted,
by his Master's warning words. "Lord," he replied proudly,
"with Thee I am ready to go to prison and to death." And
before that night had passed this proud, self-reliant, self-
confident man had denied his Lord thrice. Yes, Peter's
very strength was his weakness, and at the last it was
the discovery of his weakness that made him strong. Peter fell through his pride, through his over-weening self-
confidence, and there is one verse in his first letter which
seems to me to be addressed specially to strong and self-
reliant men; it is written in the apostle's life blood. It is
this: "Be sober, be watchful; your adversary the devil, as a
roaring lion, walketh about, seeking whom he may de-
vour."

Peter's Love

And Peter's chief virtue, his saving grace, was his love.
Peter loved the Lord with all the strength of his eager,
impetuous, enthusiastic heart. It was love that made
him leave all and follow Him at the first. It was love—

mistaken love, but still love—that would have saved Christ
from the Via Dolorosa. It was love that made him say at
the Supper, in his own impulsive way, "Thou shalt never
wash my feet"; and then, when he knew what the act
signified, "Not my feet only, but also my hands and my
head." It was love that made his sword leap out of its
scabbard in the garden. It was love that made him follow
his Lord into the judgment hall. It was love that sent him
out, after the denial, to weep bitterly. Yes, whatever
charges may be brought against Peter, this at any rate
may be said in his favor, he loved his Lord with a deep,
passionate, enthusiastic love. Pick out the most rapturous
phrases from the Book of Psalms, from the Song of Songs,
from the letters of Samuel Rutherford or the writings of
any other seraphic soul, and I will say that they are all
true of Peter. Yes, they are all true of Peter. Peter when
he gave his heart gave it utterly and altogether. "Whom
have I in heaven but thee, and there is none on earth that
I desire beside thee." Turn to the last chapter of John and
read that moving story of the conversation by the lake
between Jesus and His erring disciple. "Lovest thou me?"
said Jesus—once, twice, thrice—as if it were the one and
only vital question. "Yea, Lord; thou knowest that I love
thee," answered Peter. "Lord, You know all things, You
know this deceitful and wicked heart of mine, *You know
that I love You.*"

"Love," says Peter in his first epistle, "covereth a multitude of sins." It covered the sleep and the forsaking and
the denial. Christ had no eyes for them; He had eyes for
nothing but for His disciple's passionate and burning love.
And love still covers a multitude of sins. "Her sins," said
Christ of the woman who bathed His feet, "her sins, which
are many, are forgiven, for she loved much." And it matters not, beloved, how grievously and how often we may
have sinned, they will all be forgotten and forgiven as
Peter's were, as that woman's were, if only we love as
Peter did and as that woman did. "And I will give thee
the keys of the kingdom of heaven," said Christ to Peter.
And if you believe me, He is willing to give that same
key to us. For the key is love. Heaven is closed against

learning. Heaven is closed against rank. Heaven is closed against wealth. But heaven is open to love. The gates of the city opened wide to receive this man who, whatever his faults and failings and sins, could yet look his Lord in the face and say, "Lord, thou knowest all things; thou knowest that I love thee!"

Brethren, suffer me to ask you this plain and simple question. Do you love the Lord Jesus Christ? Are you altogether and entirely in love with Him? Do you love Him better than health, better than wealth, better than fame, better than home, better than your nearest and your best? Is your heart utterly and absolutely set upon Jesus Christ? Can you challenge Him as Peter did, and say, "Lord, thou knowest all things; *thou knowest* that I love thee"? Can you say that? Look into your hearts and tell me, can you say that? Then blessed are you, for you have the key to the kingdom of heaven; and when you leave this earth the gates of the city shall open to welcome you and all the trumpets shall sound for you on the other side.

NOTES

Beginning to Sink

George H. Morrison (1866–1928) assisted the great
Alexander Whyte in Edinburgh, pastored two churches,
and then became pastor in 1902 of the distinguished
Wellington Church on University Avenue in Glasgow,
Scotland. His preaching drew great crowds; in fact, people
had to line up an hour before the services to be sure to get
seats in the large auditorium. Morrison was a master of
imagination in preaching, yet his messages are solidly
biblical.

From his many published volumes of sermons, I have
chosen this message, found in *The Wind on the Heath*,
published in 1931 by Hodder and Stoughton, London, and
republished by Kregel Publications in 1993.

George H. Morrison

4

BEGINNING TO SINK

Beginning to sink, Peter cried, Lord, save me (Matthew 14:30).

THERE ARE TWO SIGHTS in human life which fill the heart with profound sorrow. The first is that of a person who has sunk. When we see a face made loathsome by iniquity, and think that once it was innocent and childlike; when we hear of somebody who bore an honored name, but is now in the depths of degradation, that is one of life's most piteous spectacles. It arrests even the worldly-minded who cherish no ideals for humanity; how much more must it sadden one who has anything of the vision of Christ Jesus. Men who are sunken—women who are sunken—are the heartbreak of the home and of the city. There is such infinite pathetic waste in a wasted, miserable life. But to the seeing eye and the perceiving heart there is another spectacle which is not less tragical—it is that of the man or woman who is *beginning to sink*. Beginnings are always mighty and momentous for every eye that has the power to see. Much of our knowledge and our power today springs from our modern study of beginnings. And here in our text tonight we have an instance, not of a man who has sunk into the depths, but of a man who is beginning to sink. Shall we look at him in that light for a little?

Peter's Temperament Put Him in Danger

The first thought to force itself upon me is that it was Peter's temperament which put him in this danger. He began to sink not because he was wicked; he began to sink because he was Simon Peter. The other disciples were all safe and sound. It never occurred to them to leave the vessel. They were men of sagacity and common sense, and knew the difference between land and water.

47

But Peter was reckless, headstrong, and impetuous, acting on the impulse of the moment; Peter followed the dictate of his heart, and never waited for his laggard reason. In a sense that was the glory of his character. It made him do what no one else would do. It gave him the charm of daring and enthusiasm, of that unexpectedness which always fascinates. But those very qualities that in the hand of Christ were to go to the upbuilding of the church sometimes brought him to the verge of ruin. It was only Peter who would begin to walk, and it was only Peter who would begin to sink. He was led into peril on these stormy waters because of what was self-forgetful in him. And it may be there is someone here tonight who has not sunk yet, but is beginning to sink, because he has a temperament like that. Our perils do not always reach us through our worst. Our perils sometimes reach us through our best, through what is charming in us, and delightful, and self-forgetful, and enthusiastic. And so like Peter we begin to do what the cold and calculating would never do, and then like Peter we begin to sink. That is why everyone needs to be saved not only from sin but from self. That is why God, in His holy love to save us, gave us not a message but a man. For our brightest social qualities may wreck us. A touch of genius may be our ruin. For all that is implied in that word *temperament*, we need the keeping of the Lord Jesus Christ.

Peter Began to Sink in Familiar Waters

The next thing to arrest me here is that Peter began to sink in very familiar waters. I suppose if you had asked him if he knew them, he would have replied that he knew them, every inch. Some of us, who spend our summers by the Clyde, think we are very familiar with the Clyde. And if love be at the source of all true knowledge, then indeed it may be that we know the river. But if you want a true and perfect knowledge, it is not to the summer visitor you look, but to the fisherman who was cradled by its shores. Now Simon Peter was a fisherman, and all his life had been spent beside that lake. He had played on its margins as a little child; he had known it in summer and in winter. And it was *there*, in these familiar scenes, amid what was habitual and customary, that he began to sink. There was another occasion when he began to sink, and that was in the high priest's palace at Jerusalem. He was a stranger there—in unfamiliar scenes—among men and women who knew nothing of him. Here it was different. Here he was at home. He was among those who knew him and who loved him, and here he began to sink. It is a very sad and pitiable thing when a man begins to sink away from home; when he goes away into a distant land, and forgets the God of his father and his mother. But the peril for you and me tonight is the peril of Peter on the lake of Galilee—that we begin to sink amid familiar waters. Beginning to sink in India is sad; beginning to sink at home is almost worse; forgetting the sanctuary, and the bended knee, and purity and temperance and tenderness. And if there is anyone here tonight who is beginning to sink—at home, amid those who love and pray, now is the time to cry as Peter cried, "Lord, save me, or I perish."

Peter Began to Sink After Loyal Discipleship

Another feature which I note is that Peter began to sink after loyal discipleship. He had known Christ, and had loved and followed Christ before this hour of peril on the lake. We all remember that great hour in history when Peter had been called to the discipleship. Then he had left all and followed Jesus; he had made the full surrender to the Lord. And from that hour he had companied with Jesus, and seen His miracles and heard His words, and enjoyed the infinite blessings of His friendship. No one would doubt the reality of that. That self-surrender was intensely real. And Peter loved his Lord, and knew His power, and was never happy except in His companionship. And it was after all that rich experience— that self-surrender and devoted service—that Peter on the lake began to sink. He was no raw and inexperienced youth. He was one who had heard the calling of the Master. He was no beginner in the higher life. He was a man who had done yeoman service. And the sad thing is that in every community there are men and women who begin to sink, not in their raw and inexperienced youth, but after years of discipleship and service. Sometimes it is the deceitfulness of riches which causes it. Sometimes it is growing absorption in business. Sometimes it is the constant subtle influence of one who is unspiritual in the home. Sometimes it is weariness in well-doing, and the dropping of the life to lower levels, from secret clingings that no one knows but God. No one would say such lives were sunken lives. I am not speaking of moral wrecks and tragedies. I am speaking of those who are still of good repute, still kind at home, still diligent in business. And yet one feels they have begun to sink; they are not the ones we remember in the morning; there is a different accent in their speech, and a different atmosphere around their characters. Do these simple words make anyone uncomfortable? I pray God they may be winged to the conscience. I want to waken people out of their security, as Peter was wakened on the sea of Galilee. I want them to recall their past discipleship, and to compare it with what they are tonight, and then to cry, as Simon Peter cried, "Lord, save me, or I perish."

Peter Began to Sink on a Permitted Path

Also to be noted is this fact, that Peter began to sink on a permitted path. When he began to sink he was no trespasser; he was going where Christ permitted him to go. Had our Lord cried to him across the water, You are a madman if you try to come; had He cried to him, You shall not come—on the peril of your life I bid you halt; why then we would have understood it better—we would have said it served him right to sink for then he would have been disobeying Christ, and the wages of disobedience is death. The point which I want you all to notice is that Simon Peter was not disobeying. Our Lord had not forbidden him to come. Our Lord had rather invited him to come. And so do I learn that on permitted paths—on ways that are sanctioned by the voice of heaven—it is possible now, as on the lake of Galilee, for men and women to begin to sink. There are ways that are forbidden to every child of man. God writes his flaming 'No Thorough-fare' upon them. And just for the reason that this is a righteous universe, the one who sets foot on them begins to sink immediately. But the strange thing is that even when God says 'Come,' and opens up the way that we may walk in it, even *there* it is always possible to sink. That is true of the blessedness of home. It is true of all social and Christian service. A man may preach the ever-lasting gospel, yet run the risk of being cast away. And therefore amid all our privileges, and all the gifts which God has blessed us with, "Lord, save us, or we perish."

Peter Began to Sink When He Began to Fear

Equally notable is this, too, that Peter began to sink when he began to fear. And the Scripture tells when he began to fear; it was when he took his eyes off his Lord. There is not a trace that the wind had grown more fierce while the disciple was walking on the water. It had been just as fierce, and the waves had been just as boisterous, when he had sprung from the gunwale of the boat. But then he had thought of nothing but the Master, had had eyes for nobody except the Master, and so long as that continued he was safe. Looking to Christ he could go anywhere. The very sea was as a pavement to him. Look-ing away from Christ he was as other men, and the perils that surrounded him were terrible. And then he regretted the rashness of his venture, and saw nothing around him but the seething waters, and so Peter began to be afraid, and beginning to be afraid, began to sink. That is true of every kind of life. It is true especially of spiritual life. In the perilous calling of the spiritual life, to lose heart is to lose everything. And that is why the Lord is always say-ing to us, "My son, give me thine heart"; for only in His keeping is it safe. It is a simple message—looking to Jesus—and yet it is the message of salvation. To trust in Him, and to keep the eye on Him, is the one secret of all Christian victory. And when we have failed to do so in the stress of life, as all of us, like Simon Peter, fail, then there is nothing left but to cry with Peter, "Lord, save me, or I perish."

When Peter Began to Sink the Disciples Did Not Notice

I think too we may reasonably infer that the other disciples knew nothing of all this. When Peter began to sink they never noticed it. To begin with, you must remember that all this happened about the time of daybreak. Then the waves were boisterous, and in wild confusion, so that the feet of Peter often would be hidden. And if they failed to recognize their Lord when He walked in majesty upon the waters, they were not likely to see Peter clearly. When we see someone on the point of drowning, our first instinct is to give a cry. But we have no hint of anyone crying here, save the disciple himself in his distress. And so I gather from these converging hints that when Peter began to sink into the deeps, no one saw it except he himself and Christ. I should not wonder if in this church tonight there are some people just like Simon Peter. They have not sunk yet, they are not degraded; they are just beginning to sink. Yet no one at home knows anything about it; no one suspects it or has ever dreamed of it; no one would believe it for a moment. When a person has sunk, then there is no disguising. The story is written that he who runs may read. There is nothing hidden but it shall be revealed, whether of things in heaven or things in hell. But when one is just beginning to sink it may be utterly different from that; it may be a secret between him and God. His nearest and dearest may not dream of it; his mother and father may be in total ignorance. And he may come to church, and engage in Christian service, and take his place at the communion table. And we say of him, How well he is getting on—what a fine young fellow he is turning out; and all the time, unheard and unobserved, the man is crying, "Lord, save me, or I perish." It ought to make us very tenderhearted. It ought to make us always very prayerful. There are things happening here tonight among us which we never suspect, of which we never dream. For the heart knows its own bitterness and a stranger intermeddles not therewith; but there is one who is not a stranger and *He* knows.

When Peter Began to Sink His Savior Was Near

And so I close by saying that when Peter began to sink, his Savior was not far away. Immediately He put out his hand and grasped him. How far Peter had walked upon the water the narrative of Scripture does not tell us. Shall we say fifty yards, or shall we say a hundred yards? It matters not whether fifty or a hundred. If the nearest human hand was fifty yards away, the hand of Christ was not fifty yards away; immediately He put forth His hand, and helped him. My friend, just beginning to sink, will you remember that Christ is at your side? All human help may seem very far away; remember that He is not very far away. He is near you now, near you where you sit. You need Him sorely and He is there for you. Cry out tonight, "Lord, save me, or I perish," and He will do it to the uttermost for you.

The Best House-Visitation

Charles Haddon Spurgeon (1834–1892) is undoubtedly the most famous minister of the last century. Converted in 1850, he united with the Baptists and soon began to preach in various places. He became pastor of the Baptist church in Waterbeach in 1851, and three years later he was called to the decaying Park Street Church, London. Within a short time the work began to prosper, a new church was built and dedicated in 1861, and Spurgeon became London's most popular preacher. In 1855, he began to publish his sermons weekly; today they make up the fifty-seven volumes of *The Metropolitan Tabernacle Pulpit*. He founded a pastor's college and several orphanages.

This sermon is taken from *The Metropolitan Tabernacle Pulpit*, Volume 21.

Charles Haddon Spurgeon

5

THE BEST HOUSE-VISITATION

> And forthwith, when they were come out of the synagogue,
> they entered into the house of Simon and Andrew, with
> James and John. But Simon's wife's mother lay sick of a
> fever, and anon they tell him of her. And he came and took
> her by the hand, and lifted her up; and immediately the
> fever left her, and she ministered unto them. And at even,
> when the sun did set, they brought unto him all that were
> diseased, and them that were possessed with devils. And all
> the city was gathered together at the door (Mark 1:29–33).

WE SEE BEFORE US small beginnings and grand endings.
One man is called by the voice of Jesus, and then another;
the house wherein they dwell is consecrated by the Lord's
presence, and by and by the whole city is stirred from end
to end with the name and fame of the Great Teacher. We
are often wishing that God would do some great thing in
the world, and we look abroad for instruments which we
think would be peculiarly fit, and think of places where
the work might suitably begin; it might be quite as well if
we asked the Lord to make use of us, and if we were
believingly to hope that even our feeble instrumentality
might produce great results by His power, and that our
abode might become the central point from which streams
of blessing should flow forth to refresh the neighborhood.

Peter's house was by no means the most notable building in the town of Capernaum. It was probably not the
poorest dwelling in the place, for Peter had a boat of his
own, or perhaps a half-share in a boat with his brother
Andrew, or possibly he and Andrew and James and John
were proprietors of some two or three fishing boats, for
they are partners, and they appear to have employed hired
servants (see Mark 1:20). Still Peter was not rich nor
famous, he was neither a ruler of the synagogue, nor an
eminent scribe, and his house was not at all remarkable

among the habitations that made up the little fishing suburb down by the seashore. Yet to this house did Jesus go. He had foreknown and chosen it of old, and had resolved to make it renowned by His presence and miraculous power. There hung the fisherman's nets outside the door—the sole escutcheon and hatchment of one who was ordained to sit upon a throne and judge with his fellow apostles the twelve tribes of Israel. Beneath that lowly roof Immanuel deigned to unveil Himself: God-with-us showed Himself God with Simon. Little did Peter know how divine a blessing entered his house when Jesus crossed the threshold, nor how vast a river of mercy would stream forth from his door down the streets of Capernaum. Now, dear friend, it may be that your dwelling, though very dear to you, is not very much thought of by anybody else; no poet or historian has ever written its annals, nor artist engraved its image. Perhaps it is not the very poorest in the place in which you live, still it is obscure enough, and no one as he rides along asks, "Who dwells there?" or, "What remarkable house is that?" Yet is there no reason why the Lord should not visit you and make your house like that of Obed-edom, in which the ark abode, or like that of Zaccheus to which salvation came. Our Lord can make your dwelling the center of mercy for the whole region, a little sun scattering light in all directions, a spiritual dispensary distributing health to the multitudes around. There is no reason except in yourself why the Lord should not make your residence in a city a greater blessing to it than a cathedral and all its clergy. Jesus cares not for fine buildings and carved stones; He will not disdain to come beneath your roof, and coming there He will bring a treasury of blessings with Him, which shall enrich your house, and shall ensure the richest of boons to your neighbors. Why should it not be? Have you faith to pray this moment that it may be so? How much do I wish you would! More good by far will be done by a silent prayer now offered by you to that effect than by anything which can be spoken by me. If every Christian here will now put up the supplication, "Lord, dwell where I dwell, and in so doing make my house a blessing to the neighborhood," marvelous results must follow.

I am going to speak of three things this morning. The first is, *How grace came to Peter's house*; second, *What grace did when it got there*; and third, *How grace flowed forth from Peter's house.*

How Grace Came to Peter's House

The first link in the chain of causes was that *a relative was converted.* Andrew had heard John the Baptist preach, and had been impressed. The text which was blessed to him was probably, "Behold the Lamb of God that taketh away the sin of the world." Andrew followed Jesus, and having become a disciple, he desired to lead others to be disciples too. He began, as we all ought to begin, with those nearest to him by ties of relationship—"He first findeth his own brother Simon." Beloved friend, if you are yourself saved, you should cast about you and inquire, "To what house may I become a messenger of salvation?" Perhaps you have no family of your own; I do not know whether Andrew had—he seems at the time of this narrative to have lived in a part of the same house as Peter; possibly they had each of them a house at Bethsaida, which was their own city, but they lived together when they went on business to Capernaum. Perhaps Andrew had no wife, and no children; I cannot tell. If that were so, I feel sure that he said to himself, "I must seek the good of my brother and his family." I believe, if we are really lively and thoughtful Christians, our conversion is an omen for good to all our kinsfolk. We shall not idly say, "I ought to have looked after my own children and household, if I had any, and having none I am excused," but we shall consider ourselves to be debtors to those who are kindred householders. I hope that some Andrew is here who, being himself enlisted for Jesus, will be the means of conquering for Jesus a brother and a brother's household. If there be no Andrew, I hope some of the Maries and Marthas will be fired with zeal to make up for the deficiency of the men, and will bring brother Lazarus to the Lord. Uncles and aunts should feel an interest in the spiritual condition of nephews and nieces; cousins should be concerned for cousins, and all ties of blood should be consecrated by being used for purposes of grace. Moses, when he led the people out of Egypt, would not leave a hoof behind, nor ought we to be content to leave one kinsman a slave to sin. Abraham, in his old age, took up sword and buckler for his nephew, Lot, and aged believers should look about them and seek the good of the most distant members of their families; if it were always so the power of the Gospel would be felt far and wide. The household of which Peter was master might never have known the gospel if a relative had not been converted.

This first link of grace drew on another of much greater importance, namely, that *the head of the family became a convert*. Andrew sought out his brother and spoke to him of having found the Messiah: then he brought him to Jesus, and our Lord at once accepted the new recruit, and gave him a new name. Peter believed and became a follower of Christ, and so the head of the house was on the right side. Heads of families, what responsibilities rest upon us! We cannot shake them off, let us do what we may! God has given us little kingdoms in which our authority and influence will tell for the better or the worse to all eternity. There is not a child or a servant in our house but what will be impressed for good or evil by what we do. True, we may have no wish to influence them, and we may endeavor to ignore our responsibility, but it cannot be done; parental influence is a throne which no one can abdicate. The members of our families come under our shadows, and we either drip poison upon them like a deadly upas, or else beneath our shade they breathe an atmosphere perfumed with our piety. The little boats are fastened to our larger vessel and are drawn along in our wake. O fathers and mothers, the ruin of your children or their salvation will, under God, very much depend upon you. The gracious Spirit may use you for their conversion, or Satan may employ you as the instruments of their destruction. Which is it likely to be? I charge you, consider. It is a notable event in family history when the grace of God takes up its headquarters in the heart of the husband and the father: that household's story will henceforth be written by another pen. Let those of us who are the Lord's gratefully acknowledge His mercy to us personally, and then let us return to bless our households. If the clouds be full of rain, they empty themselves upon the earth; let us pray to be as clouds of grace to our families. Whether we have only an Isaac and an Ishmael like Abraham, or twelve children like Jacob, let us pray for each and all that they may live before the Lord, and that we and all that belong to us may be bound up in the bundle of life.

Note, further, that the third step in the coming of grace to Peter's house was, that after the conversion of the brother and Peter, *there were certain others converted who were partners and companions with the two brothers.* It is a great help to a man to find godly work fellows. If he must go fishing like Peter, it is a grand thing to have a James and a John as one's partners in the business. How helpful it is to piety when Christian men associate from day to day with their fellow Christians, and speak often one to another concerning the best things. Firebrands placed closely together will burn all the more freely, coals laid in a heap will glow and blaze, and so hearts touching hearts in divine things cause an inward burning and a sacred fervor seldom reached by those who walk alone. Many Christians are called to struggle hard for spiritual existence through having to work with unbelievers; they are not only sneered at and persecuted, but all sorts of doubts and blasphemies are suggested, and these materially hinder their growth in the heavenly life. When they are brought into this trial in the course of providence they have need of great grace to remain firm under it. Beloved brother, if in your daily business you meet with none to help but many to hinder, you must live all the nearer to God, for you require a double measure of grace; but if in the providence of God you happen to be placed where there are helpful Christian companions, do not readily change that position, even though your income would be doubled thereby. I would sooner work with James and John for two hundred dollars a week than with swearers and drunkards for six hundred. You who reside with really consistent Christians are much favored, and ought to become eminent Christians. You are like flowers in a conservatory, and you ought to bloom to perfection. You live in a lavender garden, and you ought to smell sweetly. Prove that you appreciate and rightly use your privileged position by endeavoring to bring grace to your house, that it may be altogether the Lord's.

A fourth and more manifest step was taken when *Peter and his friends were drawn closer to their Lord.* The good man of the house was already saved, and his brother and companions, but by the grace of God they rose to be something more than merely saved, for they received a call to a higher occupation and a nobler service; from fishers they were to rise into fishers of men, and from rowing in their own boats to become pilots of the barque of the church. Peter was already a disciple, but he was in the background; he must come to the front; he had been more a fisherman than a disciple, but now he must be more a disciple than a fisherman. He must now follow Jesus by a more open avowal, a more constant service, a nearer communion, a more attentive discipleship, a fuller fellowship in suffering; for this he must receive an inward preparation by the divine Spirit; he was, in fact, by the call of his Lord and Master, lifted to a higher platform altogether, upon which he would abide and learn by the Spirit what flesh and blood could never reveal.

Beloved, what a difference there may be between one Christian and another. I have sometimes seen it with astonishment. I would not go so far as to say that I have seen as much difference between one Christian and another as between a Christian and a worldling, for there must ever be between the lowest grade of life and the fairest form of death a wider distinction than between the lowest and highest grades of life, yet still it is a very solemn difference. We know some who are saved—at least we hope they are—but oh, how few are the fruits of the Spirit; how feeble is the light they give; how slender is their consecration; how small is their likeness to Him whom they call Master and Lord. Thank God, we have seen others who live in quite another atmosphere, and exhibit a far different life. It is not a higher life—I hardly like that term, for the life of God is one and the same in all believers—but it is a higher condition of the life, more developed, more vigorous, more influential a condition of life which has a clearer eye, and a nimbler hand, a quicker ear, and a more musical speech; a life of health, whereas too many only know life as laboring under disease and as ready to give up the Spirit. There are Mephibosheths among the king's favorites, but give me the life of Naphtali, "satisfied with favor and full of the blessing of the Lord"; or of Asher, of whom it is written, "let him dip his foot in oil." An owl is alive though it loves the darkness, and a mole is alive though it is always digging its own grave, but give me the life of those who mount as on the wings of eagles, who live upon the fat things, full of marrow, and drink the wines on the lees well refined. These are the mighties of Israel, whose joyous energy far surpasses that of the weary and faint whose faith is feeble and whose love is cold.

Now, Peter and his friends at this time had been called from their fishing tackle and their boats to abide with Jesus in His humiliation, and learn of Him the secrets of the kingdom, which afterward they were to teach to others. They had heard the Master say, "Follow me," and they had left all at His bidding. They were in the path of fellowship, boldly pressing on at their Lord's command, so that now they had taken a grand stride in their Christian career; that is the time, beloved, when men bring blessings on their houses. Oh, I could sigh to think of the capacities which lie dormant in some Christians! It is sad to think how their children might grow up, and with God's blessing become pillars in the house of the Lord, and perhaps ministers of the Gospel, under the influence of an earnest, consecrated father and mother; but instead, the dullness, the lukewarmness, the worldliness, and the inconsistencies of parents are hindering the children from coming to Christ, hampering them as to any great advances in the divine life, dwarfing their stature in grace, and doing them lifelong injury. Friends, you do not know the possibilities which are in you when God's Spirit rests upon you, but this much is certain, if you yourselves be called into a higher form of divine life, you shall then become mediums of blessing to your relatives. Your husband, your wife, your child, your friend, and the whole of your family shall be the better for your advance in spiritual things.

Now, observe further, that at this time when the Lord was about to bless the household of Peter *He had been further instructing Peter and Andrew and James and John*, for He took them to the synagogue, and they heard Him preach. A delightful sermon it was—a sermon very full of energy, and very unlike the discourses of ordinary preachers, for it had authority and power about it; it was when they came home from synagogue, after hearing such a sermon, that the blessing descended upon the home. The best of us need instruction. It is unwise for Christian people to be so busy about Christ's work that they cannot listen to Christ's words. We must be fed, or we cannot feed others. The synagogue must not be deserted, if it is a synagogue where Christ is present. And oh, sometimes, when the Master is present, what a power there is in the word; it is not the preacher's eloquence, it is neither the flow of language, nor the novelty of thought; there is a secret, quiet influence which enters into the soul and subdues it to the majesty of divine love. You feel the vital energy of the divine word, and it is not a human word to you, but the quickening voice of God sounding through the chambers of your spirit, and making your whole being to live in His sight. At such times the sermon is as manna from the skies, or as the bread and wine with which Melchizedec met Abraham; you are cheered and strengthened by it, and you go away refreshed. My dear brother, my dear sister, then is the time to go home and take your Lord home with you. Peter and his friends had so enjoyed the great Teacher's company at the synagogue that they begged Him to abide with them, and so they went straight away with Him from the synagogue into the house. Can you do that this morning? If my Lord shall come and smile upon you and warm your hearts, do not lose Him as you go down the aisles, do not let Him go when you reach the streets and are walking home. Do not grieve Him by chitchat about worthless matters, but take Jesus home with you. If it is noonday, entreat Him to tarry with you during the heat of the day; if it is eventide, tell Him the day is far spent, and beseech Him to abide with you. You can always find some good reason for detaining your Lord. Do as did the spouse of old, when she said, "I found Him whom my soul loveth; I held Him, and would not let Him go, until I had brought Him into my mother's house, and into the chamber of her that conceived me." Is there not a sick one at home? Take Jesus home to her. Is there no sorrow at home? Entreat your Lord to come home to help you in your distress. Is there no sin at home? I am sure there is. Take Jesus home to purge it away. But, remember, you cannot take Him home with you unless you first have Him with you personally. Labor after this then; be not satisfied without it. Resolve to be His servant—to be His servant walking in the light as He is in the light, and having fellowship with Him—that I hope you are; and then, having gone so far, resolve that you will take Him to your friends and to your kinsfolk, that so your whole house may be blessed.

I desire, before I pass to the second point, to lay great stress upon this. We have an old proverb that charity must begin at home; let me shape it into this: piety must begin with you. Before you ask salvation for your family, lay hold upon it for yourself. This is not selfishness; indeed, the purest benevolence makes one desire to be qualified to benefit others, and you cannot be prepared to bless others unless God has first blessed you. Is it selfishness that makes a person stand at the fountain to fill his own cup, when he intends to hand that cup around for others to drink? Is it any selfishness for us to pray that in us there may be a well of water springing up to everlasting life, when our second thought is that out of us may flow rivers of living water whereby others may be replenished? It is no selfishness to wish that the power of the Lord may be upon you if you long to exercise that power upon the hearts cf others for their good. Look well, my friends, to yourselves; you cannot bless your children, you cannot bless your households until first of all upon yourselves rests the anointing of the Lord. O Spirit of the living God, breathe upon us, that we may live yet more abundantly, and then shall we be chosen vessels to bear the name of Jesus to others.

What Grace Did in Peter's House When It Came There

The first effect that grace produced was, *it led the family to prayer.* The four friends have come in, and no sooner are they in than they begin to speak with the Master, for the text tells us, "Anon they tell him of her"—of Peter's wife's mother who lay sick. I like that expression—I do not know whether you have noticed it—"Anon they tell him of her." Luke tells us "they besought him." I have no doubt Luke is right, but Mark is right too. "They tell him of her." It looks to me as if it taught me this—that sometimes all I may do with my sore affliction is just to tell my own dear Lord about it, and leave it to His loving judgment to act as He sees fit. Have you any temporal trouble or sickness in the house? Tell Jesus of it. Sometimes that is almost as much as you may do. You may beseech Him to heal that dear one, but you will have to say, "Not as I will, but as thou wilt," and so will feel that all you may do is to tell Jesus the case and leave it with Him. He is so gentle and loving that He is sure to do the kindest thing, and the thing which is most right to do; therefore we may be content to "tell him of her." With regard to spiritual things, we may press and be very importunate, but with regard to temporal things, we must draw a line, and be satisfied when we have told Jesus and left the matter to His discretion. Some parents may, when their children are ill, plead with God in a way which shows more of nature than of grace, more clearly the affection of the mother than the resignation of the Christian; but such should not be the case. If we have committed our way to the Lord in prayer, and have meekly told Him of our grief, it will be our wisdom to be still and watch until God the Lord shall speak. He cannot be either unjust or unkind, therefore should we say, "Let him do what seemeth him good."

Very likely this good woman, Peter's wife's mother, was herself a believer in Christ; but I venture to take her case as typical of spiritual sickness, not at all wishing, however, to insinuate that she was spiritually sick, for she may have been one of the most devoted of Christians. But now, suppose you take Jesus Christ home with you, dear friend, if you have an unconverted one in the house, you will immediately begin to "tell him of her." "They tell him of her." That is a very simple type of prayer, is it not? Yes, in some respects it is, and therefore I urge you to use it. Do not say you cannot pray for your child; you can tell Jesus of her. Do not say you cannot plead for your brother or your sister; you can go, and in a childlike manner tell Jesus about the case, and that is prayer. To describe your needs is often the best way of asking for help. I have known a person say to a man of whom he needed aid, "Now, I am not going to ask you for anything, I only want you to hear my story, and then you shall do as you like"; and if he wisely tells his story, the other begins to smile, and says, "You do not call that asking, I suppose?" Tell Jesus Christ all about it; His view of the matter will be to your advantage.

This elementary form of prayer is very powerful. The police do not allow people to beg in the streets, but I do not know that there is any law to prevent their sitting down in attitudes of misery and exhibiting holes at the knees of their trousers and bare feet staring through soleless shoes. I saw that exhibition this morning. The man was not begging, but it was wonderfully like it, and answered the purpose better than words. To tell Jesus Christ about your unconverted relative or friend may have in it a great deal of power, may be, in fact, one of the most earnest things you could do; because the absence of spoken pleas and arguments may arise from your being so burdened with anxiety that you cannot find words to say, "Lord relieve me," but you stand there and sigh under the burden, and those groanings which cannot be uttered act as urgent pleas with the pitiful heart of Christ, and cry aloud in His ear, "Lord, help me."

Telling Jesus is a simple mode of praying, but I think it is a very believing mode. It is as if they felt, "We only

need to tell the case, and our blessed Lord will attend to
it. If anon we tell Him of her, there shall be no need to
clasp His knees and cry with bitter tears for pity upon the
fevered one; for as soon as He hears, so loving is His
heart, He will stretch out His hand of power." Go to Jesus,
then, dear friends, in that spirit, about your unconverted
friend or child, and "tell him of her."

There is something very instructive about this particular case, because we are apt to think we must not tell the
Lord of the more common troubles which occur in our
family; but this is a great error. Too common? How can
the commonness of an evil put it out of the list of proper
subjects for supplication? The seaboard of Capernaum in
which Peter dwelt is said by travelers to be a peculiarly
damp, marshy, aguish, feverish place. No end of people
had the fever just around the house; but Peter and
Andrew did not argue that they must not tell the Lord
because it was a common disease. Do not let Satan get
an advantage over you by persuading you to keep back
commonplace troubles or sins from your loving Lord. Beloved, if He counts the hairs of your heads, if not a spar-
row falls to the ground without His knowledge, depend
upon it your most common trouble will be sympathized in
by Him. "In all their afflictions he was afflicted." It is a
great mistake to think you may not carry to your Redeemer the ordinary trials of the day; tell Him, yes, tell
Him all. If your child is only a common sinner, if there is
no unusual depravity in him, if your son has never grieved
you by perverseness, if your daughter has always been
amiable and gentle, do not think there is no need to pray.
If it is only a common case of the fever of sin, yet it will be
deadly in the end unless a balm be found, therefore tell
Jesus of it at once. Do not wait until your son becomes a
prodigal, pray at once! Do not delay until your child is at
death's door, pray now!

But sometimes a difficulty arises from the other side of
the matter. Peter's wife's mother was attacked by no
ordinary fever. We are told it was "a great fever": the
expression used implies that she was burning with
fever; and she was intensely debilitated, for she was

laid prostrate. Now the Devil will sometimes insinuate, "It is of no use for you to take such a case to Jesus; your son has acted so shamefully, your daughter is so willful; such a case will never yield to divine grace in answer to prayer." Do not be held back by this wicked suggestion. Our Lord Jesus Christ can rebuke great fevers, and He can lift up those that are broken down and rendered powerless by raging sin. "Wonders of grace to God belong." Go and tell Jesus of the case, common or uncommon, ordinary or extraordinary, even as they told Jesus of her.

Now, notice one or two reasons why we think they were driven to tell Jesus of her. I know the great reason, but I will mention the little ones first. I fancy they told Jesus of her, at first, because it was a contagious fever, and it is hardly right to bring people into a house that has a great fever in it without letting them know. If there is a great sin in your house, you may perhaps feel in your heart, "How can Jesus Christ come to my house while my drunken husband acts as he does?" Perhaps, more sorrowful still, the wife drinks in secret, and the husband, who sees it with deep regret, says, "How can I expect the Lord to bless us?" Or perhaps some great, sad sin has defiled your child, and you may well say, "How can I expect the Lord to smile on this house? I might as well expect a man to come into a house which is infected with typhus fever." Never mind. Tell Jesus all about it, and He will come, fever or no fever, sin or no sin.

I think perhaps they told Him of her because it would be some excuse for the scantiness of the entertainment they were likely to give. What could Peter and Andrew do at preparing a meal? The principal person in the house was ill and could not serve. We poor men are miserable hands at spreading a table, we need a Mary or a Martha to help us, or a Peter's wife, or a Peter's wife's mother. And so they say with long faces, "Good Master, we would gladly entertain You well, but she who would delight to serve You is sick." How often a family is hindered from entertaining Christ through some sick soul that is in the house. "O Lord, we would have family prayer, but we cannot; the husband will not permit it." "Lord, we would make this household ring with Your praises, but we would make one tenant of it so angry that we are obliged to be quiet." "We cannot give You a feast good Lord; we have to set before You a little as best we can, or the house would grow too hot to hold us." Never mind. Tell Jesus about it; Jesus will come and sup with you, and turn the impediment into an assistance.

Moreover, the faces of the friends looked so sad. I dare say while in the synagogue Peter had almost forgotten about his wife's mother, he had been so pleased with the preaching; but when He reached home the first question when he crossed the door was, "How is she now?" The servants replied, "Alas, master, the fever rages terribly." Down went Peter's spirits, a cloud came over his countenance and he turned to Jesus and cried, "Good Master, I cannot help being sad, even though You are here, for my wife's mother, whom I love much, is sick of a fever." That sadness may have helped Peter to "tell him of her."

But I think the grand reason was this, that our blessed Lord had such a sympathetic heart that He always drew everybody's grief out of them. People could not keep anything to themselves where He was. He looked like one who was so much like yourself, so much in all points tried like as you are, that you could not help telling Him. I exhort you that love my Lord to allow His sweet sympathy to extract from you the grief which wrings your heart, and let it constrain you to tell Him of your unconverted relative. He endured the contradiction of sinners against Himself, He loved the souls of men and women, and died for them, and therefore He can tenderly enter into the anxieties which you feel for souls rebellious and hardened in sin. Therefore, "tell him of her."

I think, however, that they told Him of her because they expected that He would heal her. Tell Jesus about your child or your friend who is unconverted, and expect that He will look upon that person with an eye of love. He can save. It is like Him to do it. He delights to do it. It will honor Him to do it. Expect Him to do it, and tell Him the case of your unregenerate friend this very day.

May I put the question all around? You have each of you, probably, someone left in your family unsaved, and you have said, "I was in hopes that this one would be converted." Have you ever told Jesus of her or of him? Oh, I hope you can answer, "Yes, I have many times"; but it is just possible you have not made a set business of it. Begin now, and go upstairs and take time every day to tell the Lord every bit about Jane, or Mary, or Thomas, or John. Wrestle with God, if need be, all night long, and say, "I will not let You go except You bless me." I do not think that many of you will be very long with that trouble to carry when you have in that manner told it to your Lord. This is what they did when Jesus came. *Immediately* they told Him of her, for the word *Anon* is really in the Greek "immediately." Directly Christ went in; they told him of her, and directly Christ went to heal her.

So the first work grace wrought in the house was it led them to pray; and, secondly, *this led the Savior to heal their sick*. He went into the chamber, spoke a word, gave a touch, lifted up the sick woman, and she was restored, and the wonderful thing was she was able to rise from the bed immediately and wait upon them. This never occurs in the cure of a fever, for when a fever goes it leaves the patient very weak, and he needs days and weeks, and sometimes months, before he recovers his wonted strength. But the cures of Christ are perfect; and so at once the patient rose and ministered to them.

Thus we see that when grace came into that house and wrought its cure *it quite transformed the family*. Look at the difference. There is the poor woman, the patient, shivering, and then again burning, for the fever is on her; she can scarcely lift hand or foot. Now look at her, she is busily serving, with a smiling face—no one more happy or healthy than she. So when God's grace comes, the one who has been the object of the most anxiety becomes the happiest of all; the sinner, saved by sovereign grace, becomes a servant of the Lord; the patient becomes the hostess.

Note the change in the rest of them. They had all been heavy of heart, but now they are rejoicing. There is no anxiety on Peter's face now, Andrew is no more troubled, the skeleton in the closet has disappeared, the sickness has been chased out, and they can all sing a gladsome hymn. The house is changed from a hospital to a church, from an infirmary to a banqueting hall. The Lord Himself seems changed, too, if change can come over Him, for, from a physician, going carefully into a sick room, He comes forth a king who has subdued an enemy, and they all look upon Him with wonder and reverence as the mighty Lord, victorious over invisible spirits. Now, I pray God that our household may be transformed and transfigured in this way: our Luz become a Bethel, our valley of Achor a door of hope, our sons of perverseness a seed to serve the Lord. If you yourselves get a fullness of grace, the next step is for your families to receive of the boundless fullness, until not one shall be soul-sick at home, but all shall be happy in the Lord, all, all shall serve Him.

How Grace Flowed Forth from the House

They could not keep the fact hidden indoors that Peter's wife's mother was cured. I do not know who told about it. Had it been in our day I would have thought it was one of the servants over the palings of the backyard, where they are so loud of talking; or perhaps some friend who came in, and was told the news. Perhaps the doctor called around to see the good woman, and, to his utter astonishment, found her up and about the house. He goes to his next patient, and says, "My business will soon come to an end; my patient who had fever yesterday has been made perfectly whole by one Jesus, a prophet of Nazareth." Somehow or other it oozed out. You cannot keep the grace of God a secret; it will reveal itself. You need not advertise your religion: live it, and other people will talk about it. It is good to speak for Christ whenever you have a fair opportunity, but your life will be the best sermon.

The story went through the town, and a poor man upon crutches said to himself, "I will hobble out to Peter's house!" Another who used to creep through the streets on all fours quietly whispered, "I will go to Peter's house and see." Others, moved by the same impulse, started for the same place. Many who had sick ones said, "We will carry our friend to Peter's house"; so the house grew popular, and, lo, around the door there was such a sight as Peter had never seen before. It was a greet hospital, all down the street patients were clamoring to see the great prophet. "Almost the whole city came around about the door." And, now, what say you to Peter's house? We began with calling it a humble lodging, where a fisherman dwelt; why, it has become a royal hospital, a palace of mercy. Here they come with every kind of complaint, lepers, and halt, and lame, and withered, and there is the loving Master, moving here and there until He has healed every one of them. The streets of Capernaum rang that night with song of joy. There was dancing in the street of a new kind, for the lame man was leaping; and the music that accompanied the dancing was of a new kind too, for then did the tongue of the dumb sing, "Glory be to God." It was out of Peter's house that all this mercy came.

Ah, friends, I would to God He would look first on Peter, and then on Peter's wife's mother, or Peter's child or relative, and then on the whole house, and then from the house cause an influence to stream forth and to be felt by all the neighborhood. "It cannot be so with my home," says one. Why not, dear brother? If you are hampered at all, you are not hampered in God; you are hampered in yourself. "But I live in a place," says one, "where the ministry is lifeless." The more reason why you should be a blessing to the town. "Oh, but I live where many active Christians are doing a great deal of good." The more reason why you should be encouraged to do good too. "Oh, but ours is an aristocratic neighborhood." They want the Gospel most of all. How few of the great and mighty are ever saved! "Oh, but ours is such a low neighborhood." That is just the place where the Gospel is likely to meet with a glad reception, for the poor have the Gospel preached to them, and they will hear it. You cannot invent an excuse which will hold water for a moment: God can make your house to be the center of blessing to all who dwell around it, if you are willing to have it so.

But the way to have it so I have described. First, you must be yourself saved, yourself called to the highest form of life, yourself warmed in heart by the presence of your Master; then your family must be blessed; and after that the widening circle around your habitation. Oh, that it might be so. I know some people who, wherever they are, are burning and shining lights; but I know some others who are lamps, but it would be difficult to say whether they are lights or not. I think I see a flicker, but I am not sure. Friends, aspire to be abundantly useful. Do you wish to live ignoble lives? Do you wish to be bound to the loathsome carcass of a dead Christianity? I abhor lukewarmness from my soul, let us have done with it! We have a very short time in which to bear our testimony, we shall soon be at rest; let us work while we can. The shadows are lengthening, the day is drawing to a close. Up! brothers and sisters, up! If you are to bring jewels to Jesus, if you are to crown His head with many crowns, up, I pray you, and labor for Him while you can.

There are some here who are unconverted. I have not spoken to them, but I have tried to set you all speaking to them. Will you do it, or shall I keep you to hear the second half of my sermon? No, I will trust you to deliver it, and may God bless you for Jesus' sake. Amen.

NOTES

Peter

Alexander Whyte (1836–1921) was known as "the last of the Puritans," and certainly his sermons were surgical as he magnified the glory of God and exposed the sinfulness of sin. He succeeded the noted Robert S. Candlish as pastor of Free St. George's and reigned from that influential Edinburgh pulpit for nearly forty years. He loved to "dig again in the old wells" and share with his people truths learned from the devotional masters of the past. His evening Bible courses attracted the young people and led many into a deeper walk with God.

This sermon is taken from *Bible Characters from the Old and New Testaments*, reprinted in 1990 by Kregel Publications.

Alexander Whyte

6

PETER

THE FOUR GOSPELS are full of Peter. After the name of our Lord Himself, no name comes up so often in the Four Gospels as Peter's name. No disciple speaks so often and so much as Peter. Our Lord speaks more often to Peter than to any other of His disciples, sometimes in blame and sometimes in praise. No disciple is so pointedly reproved by our Lord as Peter, and no disciple ever ventures to reprove his Master but Peter. No other disciple ever so boldly confessed and outspokenly acknowledged and encouraged our Lord as Peter repeatedly did; and no one ever intruded, and interfered, and tempted Him as Peter repeatedly did also. His Master spoke words of approval, and praise, and even blessing to Peter the like of which He never spoke to any other person. And at the same time, and almost in the same breath, He said harder things to Peter than He ever said to any other of His twelve disciples, unless it was to Judas.

No disciple speaks so often as Peter. "Depart from me, for I am a sinful man, O Lord. Lo, we have left all and followed thee; what shall we have therefore? Be it far from thee, Lord; this shall never be to thee. Lord, if it be thou, bid me come unto thee on the water. Lord, save me. The crowd press thee, and how sayest thou, Who touched me? thou art the Christ, the Son of the living God. To whom shall we go? thou hast the words of eternal life. Lord, it is good for us to be here; let us make three tabernacles: one for thee, and one for Moses, and one for Elias. How oft shall my brother sin against me, and I forgive him? Though all men deny thee, yet will not I. Thou shalt never wash my feet. Lord, not my feet only, but also my hands and my head. I know not the man. Lord, thou knowest all things: thou knowest that I love thee." And, to crown all his impertinent and indecent speeches, "Not so, Lord, for I have never eaten anything that is common or unclean." And then, in that charity which shall cover the multitude of sins, "Forasmuch then as God gave them the like gift as he did unto us, what was I that I could withstand God?" These are Peter's unmistakable footprints. Hasty, headlong, speaking impertinently and unadvisedly, ready to repent, ever wading into waters too deep for him, and ever turning to his Master again like a little child. "Peter was grieved because he said unto him the third time, 'Lovest thou me? And he said unto him, Lord, thou knowest all things; thou knowest that I love thee.'"

Peter's Precedence

The evangelical churches of Christendom have no duty and no interest to dispute with the Catholic Church either as to Peter's primacy among the twelve disciples, or as to his visits to Rome, or as to his death by martyrdom in that city. If the Catholic Church is satisfied about the historical truth of Peter's missionary work in the west, we are satisfied. All that can be truthfully told us about Peter we shall welcome. We cannot be told too much about Peter. And as to his primacy that Catholics make so much of, we cannot read our New Testament without coming on proofs on every page that Peter held a foremost place among the twelve disciples. In that we also agree with our friends. Four times the list of elected men is given in the Gospels; and, while the order of the twelve names varies in all other respects, Peter's name is invariably the first in all the lists, as Judas' name is as invariably the last. The difference is this: the New Testament recognizes a certain precedency in Peter, whereas the Catholic Church claims for him an absolute supremacy. The truth is this. The precedency and the supremacy that Peter holds in the Four Gospels was not so much appointed him by his Master; what supremacy he held was conferred upon him by nature. Peter was born a supreme man. Nature had, with ever-bountiful and original hands, stamped his supremacy upon Peter before he was born. And when he came to be a disciple of Jesus Christ he entered on, and continued to hold, that natural and aboriginal supremacy over other men, until a still more superior and supreme man arose and took Peter's supremacy away from him. We all have the same supremacy that Peter had when we are placed alongside of men who are less gifted in intellect, and in will, and in character than we are gifted. Peter's gifts of mind, and force of character, and warmth of heart, and generosity of utterance—all these things gave Peter the foremost place in the apostolic church until Paul arose. But Peter, remarkable and outstanding man as he was, had neither the natural ability nor the educational advantages of Saul of Tarsus. His mind was neither so deep nor so strong nor so many-sided nor at all so fine and so fruitful as was Paul's incomparable mind. And as a consequence he was never able to come within sight of the work that Paul alone could do. But, at the same time, and until Paul arose and all but totally eclipsed all the disciples who had been in Christ before him, Peter stood at the head of the apostolate, and so leaves a deeper footprint on the pages of the Four Gospels at any rate, than any of the other eleven disciples.

Peter's Personality

John was intuitive, meditative, mystical; Philip was phlegmatic, perhaps. Thomas would appear to have been melancholy and morose; while Peter was sanguine and enthusiastic and extreme both for good and for evil, beyond them all. Peter was naturally and constitutionally of the enthusiastic temperament, and his conversion and call to the discipleship did not decompose or at all suppress his true nature; the primal elements of his character remained, and the original balance and the proportion of those elements remained. The son of Jonas was, to begin with, a man of the strongest, the most willful, and the most wayward impulses; impulses that, but for the watchfulness and the prayerfulness of his Master, might easily have become the most headlong and destructive passions. "Christ gives him a little touch," says Thomas Goodwin, "of some wildness and youthfulness that had been in Peter's spirit before Christ had to do with him. When thou wast young thou girdest thyself and walkedst whither thou wouldest. But when thou art old, thou shalt stretch forth thy hands, and another shall gird thee, and carry thee whither thou wouldest not. Peter had had his vagaries, and had lived as he liked, and, Peter, says Christ to him, when thou art hung up by the heels upon a cross, there to be bound to thy good behavior, see that thou, remembering what thou wast when young, show them thy valor and thy resolution when thou comest to that conflict; and Peter remembered it, and was moved by it." Such, then, was Peter's so perilous temperament which he had inherited from his father Jonas. But by degrees, and under the teaching, the example, and the training of his Master, Peter's too-hot heart was gradually brought under control until it became the seat in Peter's bosom of a deep, pure, deathless love and adoration for Jesus Christ. Amid all Peter's stumbles and falls this always brought him right again and set him on his feet again—his absolutely enthusiastic love and adoration for his Master. This, indeed, after his Master's singular grace to Peter, was always the redeeming and restraining principle in Peter's wayward and willful life. To the very end of his three years with his Master, Peter was full of a most immature character and an unreduced and unbridled mind and heart. He had the making of a very noble man in him, but he was not easily made, and his making cost both him and his Master dear. At the same time, blame Peter as much as you like; dwell upon the faults of his temperament, and all the defects of his character, and the scandals of his conduct, as much as you like; I defy you to deny that, with it all, he was not a very attractive and a very lovable man. "The worst disease of the human heart is cold." Well, with all his faults, and he was full of them, a cold heart was not one of them. All Peter's faults, indeed, lay in the heat of his heart. He was too hot-hearted, too impulsive, too enthusiastic. His hot heart was always in his mouth, and he spoke it all out many a time when he should have held his peace. So many faults had Peter, and so patent and on the surface did they lie, that you might very easily take a too hasty and a too superficial estimate of Peter's real depth and strength and value. And if Peter was for too long like the sand rather than like the rock his Master had so nobly named him, the sand will one day settle into rock, and into rock of a quality and a quantity to build a temple with. If Peter is now too forward to speak, he will in the end be as forward to suffer. The time will come when Peter will act up to all his outspoken ardors and high enthusiasms. In so early designating the son of Jonas a rock, his Master was but antedating some of Simon's coming and most characteristic graces. His divine Master saw in Simon latent qualities of courage, and fidelity, and endurance, and evangelical humility that never as yet had fully unfolded themselves amid the untoward influences round about his life. In any case, an absolute master may surely name his own servant by any name that pleases him, especially a royal Master, for the sovereign in every kingdom is the true fountain of honor. Whatever, then, may be the true and full explanation, suffice it to us to know that our Lord thus saluted Simon, and said to him, "'Simon, son of Jonas, thou shalt be called Cephas,' which is, by interpretation, a rock."

Of the four outstanding temperaments then, Peter's temperament was of the ardent and enthusiastic order. And, indeed, a deep-springing, strong-flowing, divinely purified, and divinely directed enthusiasm is always the best temperament for the foundation and the support of the truly prophetic, apostolic, and evangelic character. For what is enthusiasm? What is it but the heart, and the imagination, and the whole man, body and soul, set on fire? And the election, the call, the experience, and the promised reward of the true prophet, apostle, and evangelist, are surely enough to set on fire and keep on fire a heart of stone. It was one of the prophetic notes of the coming Messiah's own temperament that the zeal of God's house would eat Him up. And there is no surer sign that the same mind that was found in Jesus Christ is taking possession of one of His disciples than that he more and more manifests a keen, kindling, enthusiastic temper toward whatsoever persons and causes are honest, and just, and pure, and lovely, and of good report; just as there is nothing more unlike the mind and heart of Jesus Christ than the mind and heart of a man who cares for none of these things. Let us take Peter, come to perfection, for our pattern and our prelate; especially, let us watch, and work, and pray against a cold heart, a chilling temper, a distant, selfish, indifferent mind.

Peter's Peerless Sense of Sin

Closely connected with Peter's peculiar temperament, and, indeed, a kind of compensation for being so possessed by it, was his exquisite sense of sin. We see Peter's singular sensitiveness and tenderness of spirit in this respect coming out in a most impressive and memorable way on the occasion of his call to the discipleship. Andrew was not an impenitent man. John was not a hardhearted man. But though they both saw and shared in the miraculous draught of fishes on the sea of Galilee, Peter alone remembered his sins, and broke down under them, in the presence of the power and grace of Christ. "Depart from me, O Lord, for I am a sinful man." "No; fear not," said his Master to Peter, "for from henceforth thou shalt so catch men." Peter's prostrating penitence at such a moment marked him out as the true captain of that fishing fleet that was so soon to set sail under the colors of the Cross to catch the souls of men for salvation. That sudden and complete prostration before Christ at that moment seated Peter in a supremacy and in a prelacy that has never been taken from him. And there is no surer sign of an evangelically penitent and a truly spiritual man than this—that his prosperity in life always calls back to him his past sins and his abiding ill-desert. He is not a novice in the spiritual life to whom prosperity is as much a means of grace as adversity. They are wise merchant men who make gain in every gale; who are enriched in their souls not only in times of trial and loss, but are still more softened and sanctified amid all their gains and all their comforts both of outward and inward estate. Well may those mariners praise the Lord for His goodness whose ships come home sinking with the merchandise they have made in the deep waters. But still more when, with all their prosperity, they have the broken heart to say, He has not dealt with us after our sins, nor rewarded us according to our iniquities.

Peter's Preaching

It was Peter's deep and rich temperament, all but completely sanctified, that made Peter so forgetful of himself as a preacher and so superior to all men's judgments, and so happy, to use his own noble words, to be reproached for the name of Christ. Can you imagine, have you come through any experience that enables you to imagine, what Peter's thoughts would be as he mounted the pulpit stairs to preach Judas' funeral sermon? Judas had betrayed his Master. Yes. But Peter himself, Peter the preacher, had denied his Master with oaths and curses. And yet, there is Peter in the pulpit, while Judas lies a cast-out suicide in Aceldama! "O the depths of the Divine mercy to me! That I who sinned with Judas, that I who had made my bed in hell beside Judas, should be held in this honor, and should be ministering to the holy brethren! O to grace how great a debtor!" And again, just think what all must have been in Peter's mind as he stood up in Solomon's porch to preach the Pentecost sermon. That terrible sermon in which he charged the rulers and the people of Jerusalem with the dreadful crime of denying the Holy One and the Just in the presence of Pilate. While he, the preacher, had done the very same thing before a few serving men and serving women. You may be sure that it was as much to himself as to the murderers of the Prince of Life that Peter went on that day to preach and say, "Repent, therefore, that your sins may be blotted out; since God hath sent His Son to bless you, in turning away every one of you from his iniquities." The truth is, by this time, the unspeakably awful sinfulness of Peter's own sin had completely drunk up all the human shame of it. If they who know about Peter's sin choose to reproach him for it, let them do it. It is now a small matter to Peter to be judged of men's judgment. They sang David's psalms in Solomon's porch; and that day Peter and the penitent people must surely have sung and said, "Wash me thoroughly from mine iniquity, and cleanse me from my sin. For I acknowledge my transgression, and my sin is ever before me. Restore to me the joy of thy salvation, and uphold me with thy free spirit. Then will I teach transgressors thy ways, and sinners shall be converted unto thee." And if preachers pronounced benedictions after their sermons in those days, then we surely have Peter's Solomon's-porch benediction preserved to us in these apostolic words of his: "Ye therefore beloved, seeing ye know all these things, beware lest ye also fall from your steadfastness. But grow in grace, and in the knowledge of our Lord and Savior Jesus Christ, to whom be glory both now and forever. Amen."

The Sifting of Peter

George Campbell Morgan (1863–1945) was the son of a British Baptist preacher and preached his first sermon when he was thirteen years old. He had no formal training for the ministry, but his tireless devotion to the study of the Bible helped him to become one of the leading Bible teachers of his day. Rejected by the Methodists, he was ordained into the Congregational ministry. He was associated with Dwight L. Moody in the Northfield Bible conferences and as an itinerant Bible teacher. He is best known as the pastor of the Westminster Chapel, London (1904–17 and 1933–45). During his second term there, he had Dr. D. Martyn Lloyd-Jones as his associate.

Morgan published more than sixty books and booklets, and his sermons are found in *The Westminster Pulpit* (London, Hodder and Stoughton, 1906–1916). This sermon is from Volume 1.

G. Campbell Morgan

7

THE SIFTING OF PETER

Simon Peter answered and said, Thou art the Christ, the Son of the living God (Matthew 16:16).

He began to curse, and to swear, I know not this man of whom ye speak (Mark 14:71).

THE CONTRAST IS A STARTLING ONE. It is at first sight almost inconceivable that these are the words of the same man, and yet we know that they are. Then surely we have placed them in the wrong order, and ought first to have read, "I know not the man," as language used in the days before he met the Christ; and his declaration, "Thou art the Christ, the Son of the living God," must have been made subsequently. We know, however, that this is not the case. If, indeed, they have been read in their right order a long period must have intervened between affirmation and denial. As a matter of fact, not many months had passed between the hour in which Peter rose to the height of that most wonderful confession and the hour in which he denied any knowledge of Jesus. So startling an association of texts compels us to inquire the meaning of the change which has come over Peter since that glorious and radiant hour when, amid the rocky fastnesses of Caesarea Philippi, in answer to the challenge of his Lord, he had said the one thing the heart of Christ had been waiting to hear, "Thou art the Christ, the Son of the living God."

I do not propose to consider particularly that confession of Peter, nor do I intend to dwell at any length upon the final words. I am desirous rather of asking you to consider with me the awful possibility of passing in brief time from the most blessed confession to the most dreadful denial. I think perhaps I might take another text from which to preach tonight, and if I did so it would be by way of application at the beginning as also at the close. The text would be, "Let him that thinketh he standeth take heed lest he fall." The story of Peter's denial is the story of backsliding, and it is a story which reveals the truth which we perpetually need to remember, that no man openly backslides at once. The open blasphemy is always preceded by heart backsliding. If we would understand how it came to pass that from that height of affirmation to that depth of denial a man could pass in those few brief months, we must go back to the occasion of the affirmation. We must see what happened immediately afterward, and then attempt to trace the downward progress of this man, until from mountain height we find him in the depth of the valley.

Peter's Precedent

You will remember that immediately after Peter's confession our Lord told him of His purpose concerning His church and His kingdom.

For the first time He introduced the band of disciples, in so many words, definitely and plainly to the fact of which He had been conscious all the while, that He could win His crown only by way of the cross. Immediately, while the light of the glory of the confession and the annunciation concerning the church was still about them, I find the first movement in Peter's backsliding. He said to Jesus, "Be it far from thee, Lord: this shall never be unto thee." As we hear him we are inclined to sympathize with him. We feel that we would have said exactly the same thing under the circumstances, and in all probability we would have. That, however, does not prove Peter to have been right. We may make every excuse that we will—and it is better that we should—for his limited light, for his fickleness and feebleness of character, but the fact remains that in that moment he passed out of immediate and close fellowship with his Lord.

When this man could not see Christ's method he withdrew from absolute and unquestioning loyalty to his Lord. So long as Jesus had spoken to him of building a church, Peter remained loyal; but the moment Jesus ceased to speak about keys and began to talk about a cross he was puzzled, astonished, disappointed, confused. He could not see how suffering could be the way to the throne. He could not see how his Master's going to Jerusalem and being ill-treated, and finally—for he would use no other word—murdered, could issue in the building of that glorious church to which his Lord had just made reference. He could not see how keys of any kind could be of use to him if the Master were to pass into the shadow and lose His life. Neither could I have seen it, nor could have you. So far, let us confess our perfect sympathy and fellowship with this man. It was a strange thing Jesus said to him. He had so hoped for the coming of a Deliverer. The Deliverer had come, and at last, Peter, in a moment of supreme, divine illumination, had looked into the face of the long-hoped-for Messiah and confessed Him. In his confession there was the outpouring of his soul's hope of triumph, and victory, of the breaking of chains and loosing of the captives, of the restoration of order and the setting up of the kingdom of God. I am growingly reluctant to criticize Peter, but for our own soul's profit let us see wherein lay his mistake. It lay in the fact that he was not prepared to accept his Master's estimate of necessity, was not prepared to follow his Lord simply, even when he could not understand his Lord's method. That is the common mistake of the saints. We have all made it, and therefore, sooner or later, we have found ourselves at a distance from Jesus.

The great lesson of Peter's denial is that wherever there is arrested development of Christian life there must follow deterioration of Christian character. Life must make progress to higher levels or sink lower until it pass away. I must follow Jesus Christ wholly and absolutely without question, or there will be an ever widening breach between Him and myself, until I, even I, presently shall deny Him with blasphemy over some flickering imitation fire. "Let him that thinketh he standeth take heed lest he fall."

Your affirmation of loyalty is God-inspired. Your confession of Christ is true to the deepest within you. You are perfectly honest and sincere. God help you to follow Him all the way, whether you understand Him or not. God help you at least to keep by His side when clouds almost obscure the vision of His face, for if once you let yourself question His wisdom and His word there will be distance which must increase. Let us trace this in the history of Peter. The whole subsequent story is written for us in chapter 14 of Mark's gospel. I am not going to read the whole chapter, but I desire to take you from stage to stage, that you may see how this man passed away from Jesus ever a little further, until we come to the open denial in our second text. Remember that the first step was taken when Peter shunned the cross because he did not understand it, and questioned his Lord's wisdom when He declared the method necessary to His crowning. You will find the next step in verse 29 of this chapter. "Peter said unto Him, Although all shall be offended, yet will not I." Then going on to verse 37, I read, "He," that is Jesus, "cometh, and findeth them sleeping, and saith unto Peter, Simon, sleepest thou? Couldest thou not watch one hour? Watch and pray, that ye enter not into temptation: the spirit indeed is willing, but the flesh is weak." Notice, the Lord did not call him Peter then. He went back to the old name. The next step is to be found in verse 47. "A certain one of them that stood by drew his sword, and smote the servant of the high priest, and struck off his ear." Mark is Peter's friend, and does not mention his name, but we know that the "certain one" was Peter. There we have the next step, and increased distance. I pass on to verse 54 and read, "Peter had followed afar off," and I think he seems yet a little further away from his Lord. At last he was sitting with the officers and warming himself in the light of the fire. Then, in verses 68–71, a serving maid charges him with being a Galilean, and tells him that his speech betrays him, and thrice, and finally with curses, he denies his Lord. Let us now notice the stages.

First, refusal to follow his Lord into the mystery of pain and refusal to believe that his Lord knew best. Next, boastfulness. "Although all shall be offended, yet will not I." What follows? Failure in the devotional life, inability to watch, and the cessation of prayer. Then zeal without knowledge, hastiness, the drawing of a sword, not under the command of his Master. What next? Following afar, because his Lord had rebuked him for his zeal without knowledge. Then in the chill of the night we see him warming himself over a fire which the enemies of Christ had built. And then a laughing serving maid and a lying apostle. Christ is denied, and the man of the mountain is in the depths, the man who thought he stood has fallen. The first refusal to follow Jesus has culminated in dastardly and blasphemous denial.

These things need looking at a little more closely that we may see how perfectly natural is the story. After the refusal of the cross Jesus Christ sternly rebuked Peter. "Get thee behind me, Satan: thou art a stumbling-block unto me; for thou mindest not the things of God, but the things of men." From that moment there was in the heart of Peter a consciousness that his Master was not able to trust him, a strange sense of distance between friends which is the most agonizing consciousness that can ever come either to one or the other. This man, knowing his Lord's attitude to him, will endeavor to lessen the sense of distance by loud profession. John tells us the story far more fully than it is stated in Mark. Peter said, "Lord, whither goest thou?" Jesus looked at him and said, "Whither I go, thou canst not follow me now; but thou shalt follow me afterwards." Then Peter asked, "Lord, why cannot I follow thee now? I will lay down my life for thy sake." Jesus answered, "Wilt thou lay down thy life for my sake? Verily, verily, I say unto thee, The cock shall not crow, until thou hast denied me thrice." Then Peter said, "Although all shall be offended, yet will not I." I pray you notice the principle which questioned his Master's knowledge working itself out. Peter said, in effect, "You do not know me, although You think You do. You are suspicious of me. You think I will deny You, but I will never deny You." Moreover, his boastfulness is of that most objectionable kind which puts itself into contrast with other people. "Although all shall be offended, yet will not I." In that moment Peter went further from Christ. Jesus set His face toward the cross even though there was not a single soul able to sympathize with Him. He gathered Peter, James, and John and took them to the somber shadow of the Garden of Gethsemane, and withdrawing Himself from them, told them to watch. He returned to find them asleep, and going up to the man whose profession had been so loud He said, "Simon, sleepest thou? Couldest thou not watch one hour? Watch and pray, that ye enter not into temptation." Peter boastful had become Peter unwatchful. Peter confident in himself had become the man who did not feel his need for watchfulness or for prayer, and thus in the presence of the very agony which the Lord had predicted he fell asleep. Suddenly, upon the darkness of the night there flashed the torches of the foes of Christ who had come to arrest Him. Peter was there. He had been boastful and unwatchful, and now he must make up in zeal for what he lacked in devotion. He drew his sword and smote Malchus, cutting off his ear. The Lord immediately rebuked him, "Put up again thy sword into its place: for all they that take the sword shall perish with the sword." Then we read that "Peter followed him afar off." Oh, the humanness of it. Peter said in his heart, "I can do nothing right. Whatever I say is objected to. Whatever I do is wrong. Very well then, I will drop behind." He "followed afar off." Do you see the growing estrangement? He still followed, but it was "afar off." It was a cold night, and there was a fire in the court, around which the soldiers and enemies of Christ were gathered, in all probability laughingly discussing the arrest they had made, and perhaps wondering what it all meant, for in the garden they had seen the glory flame from His eyes and had fallen to the ground. They were now perhaps laughing at their own stupidity and superstition. Peter was cold, and he warmed himself at their fire. When a man gets there it is so easy for a laughing servant girl to make him swear that he never knew his Friend at all.

The Pattern Practiced

Let us turn from the picture, keeping it in our minds only as a parable and a teaching. Let me say to you that the steps of Peter's downward career as here revealed are always the steps manifest in backsliding from the Lord. It begins at some moment when it is impossible to follow Him by sight and we decline to follow Him by faith. It begins in some crisis when He calls to something higher than we have known, and because the way to the higher level is the way of the cross and shame we draw back. Backsliding begins in some moment when we think we understand the genius of Christianity better than Jesus Christ does. You say, "Does man ever so imagine?" Ask your own heart if you have not come there often. I believe and confidently affirm that the fact that you have left the church of God and have turned your back thereto does not constitute the first thing in your backsliding. You were disobedient to the heavenly vision. Some of you have entered only today upon that first phase. The cross has confronted you, and you have shunned it. You did not believe that could be the pathway to the higher life of crowning and victory, and you have put your own thinking concerning Christian experience over against the clear command of your Lord and the word of your Lord, and immediately there begins to be distance between you.

The next thing inevitably will be boastfulness. I want to put this as practically as I know how. I am always afraid of the man who tells me he is never going to deny Christ. I have been in experience meetings, in testimony meetings, in fellowship meetings, and I have heard men say, "Whoever else turns his back upon Jesus Christ I am never going to do that." If a man should so speak in a church meeting over which I presided, he is the man I would watch over and pray for, because he is in danger. The moment a man says, "I will never leave Thee nor forsake Thee, O Christ, though everyone else shall," that man already has passed a little way out of communion with his Lord. The trembling soul in the church who says, "I walk fearfully, I am afraid lest I should grieve Him, I am afraid lest there should grow distance between me and my Lord," I need not watch over. That trembling soul will be found close to the Lord all the way.

What follows boastfulness? Always the same thing, lack of prayer and lack of watching. Young man, when you commenced your Christian life you were very regular in your habits of prayer, you were afraid of yourself and watched constantly for the coming of the Enemy. You burned bridges behind you which, alas, you are beginning to reconstruct today. You dared not walk down certain streets after you broke with evil and set your face toward following Jesus Christ, but you are beginning to frequent those old paths again. You are not quite so watchful as you were, and you excuse your lack of watchfulness by saying that there is no necessity for that carefulness and narrowness which characterize some people. There is great need for narrowness when you are walking amid precipices. The man who is sure he is safe, and who ceases to watch and drops prayer out of his life, who imagines he can live an independent life as a Christian soul, is falling already.

What follows? Again, always the same thing as in the case of Peter—zeal without knowledge. The church of God today is cursed by zeal without knowledge. This is the age of fussy feverishness, and there are multitudes of people who are attempting to overtake their lack of spiritual life by service. It is not very long since a young woman came to me and said, "I feel my Christian life is at a very low ebb. I feel that there is distance between me and my Lord, and I do not know how to improve matters. Do you not think it would be a good thing for me to take a class in the Sunday school? I replied, "A thousand times, no. In the name of God leave the children alone until you are right with God yourself." The same thing expresses itself in the invitations which sometimes reach me. People write, "Will you come and conduct a few days' special services? We want to see a deepening of our spiritual life, and we think if you came and held some evangelistic services it would help us." I invariably reply, "Get right with God first and then, if I have time, I will come." You cannot make up by doing for what you lack in being. It is well for us to remember that the last act of divine surgery which the hand of Jesus ever performed was made necessary by the blundering zeal of a distant disciple.

What follows zeal without knowledge? A slackening of the zeal, following afar off. Let us speak in the language of the day—one attendance at church on Sunday instead of two! On Sunday morning looking out to see whether it is wet, a thing you never do on Monday morning. I do not say these things to raise a smile. If they amuse you, God have mercy on you. Following afar. Following, yes, I will not deny you are following, but afar.

If you are far from Jesus you get cold, and then you want to warm yourself, and you begin doing it at the world's fires. There are all sorts of fire—they are called fires, but they are not, they are only painted. You begin to talk of narrowness. Your father did not allow you to play cards or go to the theater, but you are so chilly you want something to warm you. There are scores of men who ought to be tramping to Calvary with Christ who are playing with the Devil's fire trying to get warm. That is what I mean, nothing more and nothing less. What right had Peter at that fire? It would have been better for him to have been starving outside in the cold night than getting warmth there. The world knows you. You cannot drop the speech of Jesus all at once. You are of the same country and kin as He is, and at painted fires. Go back to Him. Walk with Him. Talk to Him. Serve Him. Let Him talk to you. Then, suddenly, in the midst of the chilliness, you will say, "How my heart burns within me when He talks to me by the way." Or are you following afar off? Is the old first love, the love of betrothal and espousal gone? Press back to Him. It is you who have changed, not He. It is your love that has cooled, not His. Press back to Him, and you will find Him ready to receive you even now. Or are you among the number of those who are neglecting prayer in order to do more work for God? Do less work for God and pray more. Are you neglecting the hour of devotion because you have so many things on hand in connection with the Christian church? Get some of the things out of your hands and hold your hands empty to heaven for a longer space, I charge you. I often think it would be a blessed thing for the church of God if for a little while she attempted to do less and worshiped more.

The doing, in the end, would be not less, but more and mightier. I pray you hasten back to the mountaintop, the place of quietness and seclusion, of keen watchfulness and prayerfulness, which marks your sense of dependence. Perhaps you have not come so far as this, and are a little angry with me tonight. You are saying, "Why does the preacher so talk to us? We shall never do this thing. I am never going to deny Christ." Is that the language of your heart? Then it proves you are a distance from Him. The nearer a man is to Christ, the more conscious he is of his own frailty, and the more is he possessed of strength, though he hardly knows it. The nearer a man lives to Jesus Christ, the more acutely conscious is he of distance between him and his Lord by reason of his Lord's superior strength and his own frailty, and the more he presses closely to Him.

Are you shunning some cross which His will appoints, setting up your own estimate of His will and method as against His? Do not shun the cross. He sees the cross as a means of grace. It is an old word and we have made a proverb of it. We used to engrave it upon bookmarkers— "No cross, no crown!" It is the whole philosophy of Christian life. Remember the cross there is not His cross, but your cross. Did He not say, "If any man would come after me, let him deny himself, and take up his cross daily, and follow me." It is when a man shuns the cross that he passes out of intimate fellowship and begins the downward course.

My final word is that already twice said. Wherever you may be, you need go no farther. Turn back to Him and to His love, back to His heart ere you rest tonight, and you will find Him the same loving, almighty Savior.

NOTES

The Turning Again of Peter

George Campbell Morgan (1863–1945) was the son of
a British Baptist preacher and preached his first sermon
when he was thirteen years old. He had no formal training
for the ministry, but his tireless devotion to the study of
the Bible helped him to become one of the leading Bible
teachers of his day. Rejected by the Methodists, he was
ordained into the Congregational ministry. He was
associated with Dwight L. Moody in the Northfield Bible
conferences and as an itinerant Bible teacher. He is best
known as the pastor of the Westminster Chapel, London
(1904–17 and 1933–45). During his second term there, he
had Dr. D. Martyn Lloyd-Jones as his associate.

Morgan published more than sixty books and booklets,
and his sermons are found in *The Westminster Pulpit*
(London, Hodder and Stoughton, 1906–1916). This sermon
is from Volume 1.

G. Campbell Morgan

7

THE TURNING AGAIN OF PETER

From that time began Jesus to show unto His disciples that He must go unto Jerusalem, and suffer many things of the elders and chief priests and scribes, and be killed, and the third day be raised up. And Peter took Him, and began to rebuke Him, saying, Be it far from Thee, Lord: this shall never be unto Thee (Matthew 16:21–22).

Verily, verily, I say unto thee, When thou wast young, thou girdedst thyself and walkedst whither thou wouldest; but when thou shalt be old, thou shalt stretch forth thy hands, and another shall gird thee, and carry thee whither thou wouldest not. Now this He spake, signifying by what manner of death he should glorify God. And when He had spoken this, He saith unto him, Follow Me (John 21:18–19).

LET US READ these passages again, omitting all save the actual words of Peter as recorded in the first, and those of Jesus as recorded in the second. "Be it far from Thee, Lord; this shall never be unto Thee." "Verily, verily, I say unto thee, when thou wast young, thou girdedst thyself, and walkedst whither thou wouldest: but when thou shalt be old, thou shalt stretch forth thy hands, and another shall gird thee, and carry thee whither thou wouldest not. . . . Follow Me."

Last Sunday evening I spoke to you on the subject of the sifting of Peter. This evening we turn our attention to our Lord's method in restoring him. Ere we trace the stages in his turning again, I would notice the significance of the two passages we have read. The one reveals the first movement of Peter out of harmony with his Lord, when for the first time Jesus definitely told His disciples that He must needs go to Jerusalem and suffer and be killed, and the third day be raised up. Peter stood in the presence of the announcement astonished and afraid, and instead of following his Lord, though unable to understand

97

Him, he said, "Be it far from Thee, Lord: this shall never be unto Thee." The Master immediately rebuked him in the sternest terms, "Get thee behind me, Satan: thou art a stumbling-block unto me: for thou mindest not the things of God, but the things of men." When I come to the scene at the seashore, and to the final movement in it, I hear Jesus saying to him, "When thou wast young thou girdedst thyself, and walkedst whither thou wouldest; but when thou shalt be old, thou shalt stretch forth thy hands, and another shall gird thee, and carry thee whither thou wouldest not. . . . Follow Me." Thus Jesus brought Peter back to the cross, to his own cross. Peter failed in following when his Lord's cross was presented to him. He was restored to following when his own cross overshadowed his life. Yet there are many stages between that movement out of fellowship and that perfect restoration. This evening, to magnify His grace and to attempt to set forth the patience and persistence of the Lord in seeking after and restoring His wandering ones, I shall ask you to follow me as I attempt to trace the stages of the restoration, for the man turning his back upon the cross is not immediately transformed into a man who consents to the cross and comes presently to glory in the fact that he is counted worthy to suffer shame for his Master's name. There was much—I speak it very reverently, although the *much* of human speech is an awkward word to use of the divine activity—there was very much for the Master to do for this man. While we shall see Peter all through our study tonight, I pray you attempt to fix your eyes not on him, but on the Lord, marking the method of His mercy and His patience, how He commenced to make a highway home for this Peter, and how He went after Peter persistently until He set his feet once more upon the broad highway of His commandment, and commissioned him to all the toil of the coming years.

Last Sunday evening we were able to trace the downward steps of Peter in Mark 14. In order to follow consecutively the method of the Master's restoration we cannot confine ourselves to one chapter, but shall attempt to follow it by turning to different passages in the Gospel writings. The first to which I shall draw your attention is to be found in Luke 22:31–32. Here the Master is speaking to Peter, and says to him (and here I very deliberately use the marginal rendering), "Simon, Simon, Satan hath obtained you by asking, that he might sift you as wheat: but I made supplication for thee, that thy faith fail not: and do thou, when once thou hast turned again, stablish thy brethren." That is the first step in Peter's restoration. The "you" is plural and the reference is to all the disciples: "but I made supplication for *thee*, that *thy* faith fail not." That is singular and personal and immediate. This does not mean that Jesus did not pray for the rest, but it is a special word for Peter. While He tells Peter that he, in common with all the rest, has been obtained by Satan for sifting, He singles Peter out because he is especially in peril.

Step One: A Prayer

The first step our Lord took toward the restoration of this man then was that of storing up in his mind words which would be of service to him in the days to come. In one flash of light He revealed a most startling situation. A human soul stands between two forces, the forces of evil and of good. "Satan hath obtained thee by asking . . . but I made supplication for thee." Satan has been asking about this man. Jesus has been asking about him. Over against the asking of Satan, Jesus has put His own asking. All that will pay for further consideration, and we postpone it. What I now want you to notice is that Jesus told Peter He had prayed for him that his faith should not fail. Was that prayer answered? Certainly. You say, "But his faith did fail." Never. He denied his Lord, Yes, and believed in Him all the time. What did fail? His courage, his hope, his obedience, not his faith in the Person. The faith of the disciples of Jesus never failed. The two men walking to Emmaus had lost hope and courage and confidence, but not faith in Him. They had lost faith, in the sense of having certain convictions about Him weakened, but they had not lost their faith in Him personally. They thought He had been mistaken. They thought He had failed. They said, "We hoped that it was He which should redeem Israel." Their use of the verb *to hope* was in the past tense. They had lost their hope, but they said He "was a prophet mighty in deed and word," and that suggests that they still believed in Him. The faith which saves is not faith in anything heard about Jesus, but faith in Jesus. Peter's faith never failed. His courage failed, his obedience failed, his hope died out; but he never lost his faith in Jesus. I think the hour came when he thought his faith had failed. A great many people come there. But Jesus had prayed for Peter before his denial, before the outward and evident manifestation of the inner heart backsliding. He had taken an advance march against the Enemy, had garrisoned the soul of His child against all the sifting of hell. Thank God, that is my Savior. I hope He is your Savior, dear heart. So He begins His method of restoration.

Step Two: A Look

In this same 22d chapter of Luke we find the next step in verse 61. "And the Lord turned and looked upon Peter." Just a look. I cannot interpret it. There was no theology in it. There were tears in it. Have you ever asked yourself quietly when you were alone how Jesus looked at Peter? I think I know how I would have looked at him. I am very much afraid, from what I know of my own heart, that if my bosom friend had denied me in answer to the give and take of a servant girl and the mockery of brutal soldiers just when I most needed him, when my life was being sworn away, my look might have been one of anger. Jesus did not look that way. I know He did not. If there be anything of His grace in my heart I might not have looked in anger, but I think the highest thing that could ever have been said of my looking would be that I looked reproachfully at Peter. Do you think Jesus did that? Do you think that day in the judgment hall He looked back where Peter stood by the fire cursing and swearing, and there was something in His look which said, "Peter, is that you? Can you add to my sorrow? Can you help to break my heart?" I do not think He looked like that. I think He was too self-emptied. I do not think there entered into the thinking of Jesus the sorrow caused to Him by His friend's denial. I think His was a look aflame with the pity of God. I think it was a look ineffable in its tenderness, which said to Peter, not, "What sorrow art thou causing Me," but "What sorrow art thou causing thyself?" I think it was a great look of compassion, full of tenderness divine. Overwhelmed with personal sorrow, He forgot His sorrow in pity for the grief which this foolish man was bringing to his own heart. That interpretation may not be correct. Therefore I simply remind you of what happened and ask you to find out when you are alone what the look meant. Of this at least I am sure, that look broke Peter's heart. I do not think a look of anger would have done that. I almost question whether a look of reproach would have done it. But, oh, the pity of those eyes! The unveiling of God's compassion in those eyes! Peter hurried out into the night. He is coming home. A man is always coming home when he quits the world's fire for the dark night in penitence. There are many tears and sighs and dark hours to go through, but he is coming home. My dear man, are you brokenhearted because you have denied your Lord? Have you quit the world's fires? Are you very dark and desolate and lonely in this house tonight? You are on the way home.

Step Three: A Personal Message

What is the next thing? We turn to chapter 16 of Mark's gospel and find it in the 7th verse. An angel is speaking to the women, and in the midst of his speaking we hear these words: "Go, tell His disciples . . . He goeth before you into Galilee: there shall ye see Him, as He said unto you." I am so glad you have Bibles and have noticed the omission. "Go, tell His disciples *and Peter*." I do not know how much that means to you. Have you ever thought how much it meant to Peter? The message was all wrapped up in two words, one of which was his own name, and the other the little conjunction which linked him to the other disciples—"and Peter." Imagine for a moment, if you can, what Peter had been passing through.

Think of the judgment hall where they swore His Lord's life away, and condemned Him to the brutal death on the cross. Think reverently how they had buffeted Jesus and bruised Him: and think all the while, if you would understand it, from Peter's standpoint. Think how they nailed Jesus to the cross, how they watched Him die, and remember that Peter was saying in his heart, "He is dead, and the last thing He ever heard me say was that I did not know Him." May God deliver every man and woman in this house from the unutterable sorrow of losing a loved one, which loved one last heard you say an unkind thing. If you said an unkind word as you left home tonight, get up and go home and put it right. It may become the agony of your life. Think of it in Peter's case. Cannot you hear him saying, "I denied Him with curses, and swore I did not know Him, and He heard me, and He looked, and I have never had a chance to say another word. He is gone. He is dead. Those eyes cannot look at me now. Those lips cannot speak to me. The hand that leaned on me as we walked will never rest on my shoulder again. He is dead." I have sometimes tried to go with Peter through those days and nights after the Lord looked at him, and I cannot help feeling that they were days and nights of unutterable sorrow.

It is the resurrection morning. The women are early there. They have seen a vision of angels, and are coming with swift steps to the disciples. Peter is somewhere among them, on the outskirts. He felt he did not belong to them. They had all run away, but he alone had denied his Lord. The women are delivering their message and Peter is listening with the rest. Suppose the women had said, "We have seen an angel who told us to tell His disciples that He has gone into Galilee, and we shall see Him there." Peter would have said, "That is not for me. He wants to meet the disciples, but I have denied Him. I have cut myself off from the disciples. I have put myself outside." The Lord knew it. The Master of angels, while yet in the spirit world, charges His angel to tell the women to deliver His message to the disciples *and Peter*. The women come to the disciples and say, "The angel said we were to tell His disciples *and Peter.*" Immediately there is new hope in the heart of that man, or I do not know human nature. I am not sure that the sorrow did not grow. There is nothing breaks a man's heart like the sign of forgiveness. If I have wronged you and you are hard with me, I shall be sorry; but if you are kind to me you will break my heart. Peter is saying, "He has something to say to me. I wonder what." So the Lord has taken another step toward bringing him home. He has sent him a message.

Step Four: A Personal Meeting

The next step in the restoration is found in Luke 24:33–34, "And they rose up that very hour, and returned to Jerusalem, and found the eleven gathered together, and them that were with them, saying, The Lord is risen, and hath appeared to Simon." The Lord had revealed Himself to the two men walking to Emmaus, and they hastened back to Jerusalem with the news that they had seen Him, and found the Eleven gathered together, and it was the Eleven who said, "The Lord is risen, and hath appeared to Simon." I do not know how you are going to place that chronologically. I am not sure whether He appeared to Simon before He walked to Emmaus with the two men, or somewhere in the interim between His breaking of bread with them and their getting back again to Jerusalem. I think probably it was before the walk to Emmaus. When the two men from Emmaus got back to Jerusalem to tell what they had seen they found all the disciples filled with wonder and saying, "The Lord is risen, and hath appeared to Simon." Where He appeared to Simon I do not know. What He said to Simon, I dare not tell you dogmatically. There is no record of it. The fact that He appeared to Simon is chronicled, and it was so important that Paul knew about it, and when he mentioned the appearances which demonstrate resurrection, he included this, "He appeared to Cephas." This is the Lord's next step in bringing Peter home, a private, lonely interview. I am so glad I do not know where it happened. I am so thankful there is no record of what passed between them. There are things which pass between a penitent soul and Christ which no third man ought to hear. When Jesus is restoring a soul He is sure to get that soul alone somewhere, and when all others—apostles, prophets, and teachers—are outside, He will talk with that soul face-to-face. So He talked with Peter. I wonder if you will be patient while I try to imagine one thing He said to Peter. I am almost reluctant to do it. I would not do it if I had not had some such experience myself. I think, among other things, there would be something like this: "Peter, I told you I must go to the cross." Only you must not imagine that Christ said it as you say to people, "I told you so." It was not said in a triumphant tone, to rebuke him. "You did not want me to go to the cross; but, Peter, I have been to the cross, and by My blood your sins are forgiven." I think He said something like that. I think Peter learned in that private interview the meaning of the cross. I think he felt the virtue of the cleansing blood. I think in that hour Peter found out the folly of his own mistake and the wisdom of his Master's method.

Thus finally we come back to John 21, in which we have the last movement in the restoration of this man. May I remind you of the steps already taken? First, Jesus prayed for Peter. Second, He looked at Peter. Third, He sent Peter a message. Fourth, He had a private interview with Peter; and now, in the story of the events which took place on the shore of the lake, you will find the fifth, sixth, and seventh steps. What is the fifth? He challenges Peter's love. The sixth, He gives Peter back his work and commissions him. The seventh, He puts the cross in front of Peter and says, "Follow Me."

Step Five: A Challenge

First, He challenges Peter's love. There is such wonderful fitness in all our Lord does, and in all His ways. I know it is an old story. We have often read it, but it will not harm us to look at it once more. There are contrasts and similarities in this story which I think are very wonderful. Peter had denied the Lord in the city. Jesus takes him away from the city, with its rush and roar and all its seductions, to the sea. Peter had denied Him just past midnight. Jesus meets Peter there by the sea in the early morning hour, just when men are beginning to see clearly, and from the boat they looked and saw a stranger on the shore. Peter had denied Him by a fire which Jesus' enemies had built. Jesus builds a fire now for Peter, and calls him to confess Him over that fire. Peter had thrice denied Him. Thrice our Lord calls him to confess. Is there any picture in all the Bible more full of beauty? How does Christ begin? Is this a formal court to which He brings Peter? No. It is an informal breakfast. No ecclesiastical commissioners these before whom Peter is arraigned, but fishermen with the tang of the sea and the weariness of the night upon them, and the hunger of robust physical health. The risen Christ has built a fire, and cooked fish and prepared bread, and He said to them, "Come and break your fast." He waited on them. You did not miss that, did you? He made them sit down and He waited on them. When they had broken their fast, and the light of the morning was all about them, the fire glowing there, and no sense of chilliness, Jesus looked at His servant and said, "Simon, son of John, lovest thou Me?" It is somewhat wearisome and academic, yet one must point out the difference between these words translated "love." When Jesus asked that question He used a high word, which indicates love upon an intellectual plane. "Lovest thou Me with the love of illuminated intelligence?" That is not what He said, but that is what is in the word. Peter did not use that word but took a lower word, a warmer word, an emotional word. "Yea, Lord, Thou knowest that I fondly love Thee."

Step Six: A Commission

Immediately Jesus said to him, "Feed My lambs." Then once again He said, "Simon, son of John, lovest thou Me?" And still the word is the high word with all the light of God upon it. Peter again got down to his lower word, a very beautiful word nevertheless. "Yea, Lord, Thou knowest that I fondly love Thee." Peter dared not climb to Christ's high word. Then listen, the third time the Lord came down in great grace to Peter's lower word, and said,

"Simon, son of John, fondly lovest thou Me?" That is why Simon was grieved. Not because Jesus asked him three times if he loved Him, but because the third time He descended to the lower word. He did not like His Lord to come down, but he has learned such a lesson that he dared not climb to the high word. "Lord, Thou knowest all things; Thou knowest that I fondly love Thee." Did Peter ever climb to the high word? Yes. Read his epistles. He never uses the lower word, always the high word of Jesus. That morning by the lake he just kept on the level of the love he knew he possessed. Mark the contrast in this man. A little while ago he had said to Jesus, "Thou dost not understand me. Though all should forsake Thee, I will not." Now he says, "Lord, Thou knowest all about me. Thou knowest all things, Thou knowest that I love Thee." A little while ago, over the fire the enemies of Jesus had built, Peter had denied Him thrice. Now, in the sunlight of the morning, in the warmth of the fire Christ had built, Peter thrice confessed Him, and every time Jesus restored him to his work, and so brought him back into full and perfect fellowship and communion.

I am bound to stop for a moment to say, in God's name get away from the fires Christ's enemies are building for warmth. He knows how to build fires. There is in your nature no demand that He cannot supply. You want enthusiasm, passion, fire? Let Him build it and kindle it and inspire it. Man, if you go to the world's fires, you will burn your passion out until it is nothing but ashes and dust upon the world's highway. Go to Christ's fires and He will take your passion and make it flame and burn. That seems to me to be the value of this fire which Jesus built. He is saying to men for all time, "If the morning is chill and you want warmth I can build your fire." So He has called for His child's confession, and has given him back his work by the fire which He Himself has built.

Step Seven: A Cross

There is one other step. He looked at Peter once more and said, "Follow Me." "When thou wast young, thou girdedst thyself, and walkedst whither thou wouldest: but when thou shalt be old, thou shalt stretch forth thy hands, and another shall gird thee, and carry thee whither thou wouldest not." I think we may interpret that, "When you were young you were your own master, and had your own way, and went whither you would. You made your own choices and decisions. Presently, when you are old, when you most need comfort and help, there is a desolating experience waiting for you, Peter. You will stretch out your hands and another will gird you and carry you whither you would not." John listened, and he understood these mystic sentences better than any other man, so he put in a parenthesis, "Now this He spake, signifying by what manner of death he should glorify God." Accepting that word of John as true, when Jesus said these words to Peter He meant to say to him, "When you were young you had your own way. You have been impulsive, girding yourself in great independence; but there is an hour coming when someone else will gird you, and bind you and crucify you." It is as clear a picture of the cross as came to Peter at Caesarea Philippi. But that is not all Christ says. Do not go away and think that is all. "Follow Me." What does that mean? "Peter, you were afraid of my cross. I have endured the cross. I have despised the shame. I have risen from among the dead. I am your Lord and Master. Peter, you are coming to the cross. Follow Me. Come My way. My cross leads to My crowning. Your cross will lead to your crowning. My dark day of shame issued in My glad Easter morning of glory. All the perils of your pathway and its pain but lead you out to the kingdom and to life. Follow Me." And Peter followed Him. He was not changed into an angel, for the very next thing he tried to do was to interfere about John. "What shall this man do?" He is still the same impetuous, impulsive Peter, but he has heard the supreme word. I take his epistles up presently and read them and find in all of them the glory of his knowledge of his Lord. I find in all of them his consciousness of the infinite meaning of the cross. I find in all of them his consent to the cross and his abandonment to its claims, and I find in all of them his triumphant, glorious victory.

An Appeal

The Savior who brought Peter back is waiting for you. How shall I say it? Now the crowd hinders me as it always does. I cannot say it, but thank God that while I am witness of these things so also is the Holy Spirit. Listen now to the voice of the Spirit who is speaking in your heart. Far away are you? Brokenhearted, disappointed with yourself? You have denied Him and He has looked at you. He sends you a message, He is at your side. He wants to talk to you all alone. Let Him. There has been no cooling of His love, no failure in His faithfulness. Where are you, man? Wandering yet? Are you brokenhearted and disappointed? You have gone very far from Him. You have been very mean toward Him. You have dragged His name in the dust, but still His arm is about you. His hand is on your head, and it is a pierced hand. He presses you to His heart, against His wounded side. Trust Him. God help you to trust Him. At last, by the way of the cross, He will bring you also to the crowning. Is there distance between you and your Lord? Cancel the distance. Get back to Him. His love is stronger than death, mightier than the grave. No waters can quench it, and He loves you. I have no other word to say. God help you to see it for yourself, and to obey it by returning to Him now.

NOTES

Peter's Three Calls

Charles Haddon Spurgeon (1834–1892) is undoubtedly the most famous minister of the last century. Converted in 1850, he united with the Baptists and soon began to preach in various places. He became pastor of the Baptist church in Waterbeach in 1851, and three years later he was called to the decaying Park Street Church, London. Within a short time the work began to prosper, a new church was built and dedicated in 1861, and Spurgeon became London's most popular preacher. In 1855, he began to publish his sermons weekly; today they make up the fifty-seven volumes of *The Metropolitan Tabernacle Pulpit*. He founded a pastor's college and several orphanages.

This sermon is taken from *The Metropolitan Tabernacle Pulpit*, Volume 12.

Charles Haddon Spurgeon

9

PETER'S THREE CALLS

And the two disciples heard him speak, and they followed Jesus (John 1:37).

And Jesus, walking by the sea of Galilee, saw two brethren, Simon called Peter, and Andrew his brother, casting a net into the sea: for they were fishers. And he saith unto them, "Follow me, and I will make you fishers of men" (Matthew 4:18–19).

And . . . he . . . called unto him his twelve disciples. . . . the first, Simon, who is called Peter (Matthew 10:1–2).

PERHAPS YOU ARE AWARE that there has always been a certain set of persons who have tried to disprove the Gospel narrative by picking out what they suppose to be discrepancies, especially in the statements of Matthew and Luke. Four independent persons have each given us a separate story of the life of Christ, each story being written with a distinct object. Of course, from the fact that each one was written with a distinct object, it was natural that one evangelist should give more attention to certain points in the history of Christ than the others, and it was natural for his eye to be fixed upon those things which most concerned the point which he had in hand, and for his ear to be most quick to catch those words which had a relation to the object he was driving at throughout the whole of his gospel. Now, these divergences and differences have been so many pegs upon which quibblers have hung their quibbles, and these men have constantly been saying, "How do you reconcile Matthew with John in a certain place, or how do you reconcile Mark, in such another place, with Luke?" Now, it is not always easy to harmonize the testimony of four perfectly honest witnesses upon the same subject. I will venture to say that if there should be a simple accident upon the railway, and four persons present were to give their accounts of it with rigid exactness, yet they would each one be likely to mention some point not mentioned by the others, and, moreover, differ upon the points which they notice in common. Although we might be morally convinced that they all spoke the truth, yet it would be difficult to put the story together so as to make a harmonious whole of it. Sometimes it is not easy to put the stories of the evangelists together, and many of the "Gospel Harmonies," so called, which have been produced by very admirable writers, are not quite correct, but show at once the difficulty attaching to that which some brethren have been trying to attempt, and which perhaps will never be fully carried out, namely, the making of it into one harmonious idyll.

It so happens, however, that the difficulty in the case before us is no difficulty at all. John tells us that Peter was called by Christ through the preaching of John the Baptist, who bore witness that Jesus was the Christ, the Messiah. Matthew, on the other hand, tells us that Peter and his brother were fishing, that Christ was walking by the lake of Galilee, and that as He passed by He saw these men fishing, called them by name, and said, "Follow me." Now, the key to the whole may be found in the fact that there was yet a third call, and that afterward Jesus called, not Peter and Andrew alone, but the whole twelve of his disciples, and set them apart to be apostles; and so we gather from this last call that the other two might perhaps have been different and distinct from each other. Coming to look at the subject we find that the first call was the call at Peter's conversion, which called him to be a disciple while still at his daily avocation; the second was the call of Peter, not to be a mere disciple, but to be an evangelist; and the third was the call of Peter, not to be an evangelist or a common servant of the Master, but to be a leader, to take a yet higher grade, and to become one of the twelve who should be associated with Christ as the founders of the new system of religion, and witnesses of the life of Christ Himself.

Three Calls Under Consideration

I want you, then, just for a moment to bear in mind that we have under our consideration three calls: (1) The first is that which Christ gave to Peter when He called him out of darkness into marvelous light, blessing to him at first the testimony of John, and then by manifesting Himself to him; (2) the second is the call by which the servant already converted, already willing, is bidden to put himself into closer relationship with his Lord, to come out and be no longer a servant whose allegiance is true but not manifest, but to show that fealty by following his Master; (3) and the third call is that which the Savior gives only to a few whom He has picked out and chosen to do some special work, who shall have fellowship with Him more closely still, and become captains in the ranks of "the sacramental host of God's elect."

We shall speak of these three calls in the order in which they occur. Very briefly I shall go through the subject, speaking at length about the second call which Peter received.

The Personal Call to Be a Disciple

These three calls are given in a certain order. Observe where it begins. Peter was not called to be an evangelist before he was called to be a follower. Christ begins by first teaching us our own need of Him, and our own sin, and then revealing Himself to us as the Lamb of God who takes away the sin of the world. It is a presumption—what if I say an accursed treason—against the Majesty of the great Head of the church if any man pretends to reverse this order. You must first be called yourselves into Christ before you may dare to even so much as think about being called into the ministry or into the service of Christ. You cannot serve Him until first of all you have learned to sit at His feet. Before you can serve God you must have a new heart and a right spirit. The blind eye is not fit for the service of Christ. The eye must be illuminated, the understanding must be instructed. That stubborn will of yours cannot bear the yoke of Christ; it must be subdued. "Ye must be born again." Should there be some among you here tonight who are teaching in Sunday schools, distributing tracts, or in any other way are trying to serve God, and yet are not yourselves saved, I would very affectionately, but with great earnestness, entreat you to consider that you are reversing the natural and proper order of things. Your first business is at home, in your own soul and your own heart. I will not apply to you the words of the prophet, "Unto the wicked God saith, What hast thou to do to declare my statutes?" But I think there is a spirit in those terrible words which might well have an application to you. How can you be a guide until you are first able yourself to see, for "if the blind lead the blind, they shall both fall into the ditch"? How can you, diseased and leprous, begin to heal others, for it shall be said to you, "Physician, heal thyself." How can you when the beam is in your own eye go abroad to point out the beams and the motes which are in other men's eyes? Oh! take care, take care lest this very service to Christ, as you think it, be an injury to you, for you may serve Christ after a sort until you begin to think that you do so much, and do it so well, that you must be a Christian. You may spin for yourself a robe which shall seem sufficient to cover you withal, and you may go and dress in this cobweb, this mere figment of a fictitious righteousness, and persuade yourself that you are wearing the robe of Christ's righteousness, whereas you shall be found at the last to be naked, and poor, and miserable. Oh! I pray you to understand those meaning words, "Behold the Lamb of God." Behold Him for yourselves, see Him for yourselves. Do not talk about being a fisher of men; do not speak of being a servant whose loins are girt, and whose lamp is trimmed, until first you have become as a little child, for unless you so become you cannot enter into the kingdom of heaven.

The Call into Active Service

But, dear friends, after the first call has been received, it is very delightful to observe the Christian receiving the second. He is called into active service. Simon Peter became a disciple, but all that he meant by that was, "I acknowledge Jesus of Nazareth to be the Messiah," and he went away and continued with his good brother in the fishing business. It never, perhaps, entered into his head that he was to do anything more than to cultivate a quiet, peaceful faith, and walk in a life consistent therewith. But on a sudden he sees this famous man of Nazareth walking by the seaside, who addresses him by name, and says to him, "Follow me"; and in a moment, putting down his net and leaving his relative, with his two companions, James and John, equally famous in the battle-roll of Christian heroes, he left all to follow Christ.

Now, I may have some here tonight who are saved. You are the disciples of Jesus, but I regret to know that He has not yet been seen by you as calling you into His service. You have joined the church, and you have been baptized into the faith of Christ, and so far it is good; but as yet it has not struck you that you are to be actively engaged for Christ. Now, it is not in my power to call you to the service, nor to indicate to you what special form that service shall take; but, my dear friends, I do pray that you may have another revelation of the Lord Jesus yet more full and bright, and that He may say to you, "Come, man, thou art not thine own; thou art bought with a price; serve Me; arise, gird up thy loins, and wait upon the Lord." I trust that He may lay His hand upon you tonight, and say to you as He did to the assembled Twelve, "As my Father hath sent me into the world even so send I you"; may you have grace to obey the mandate, and though it may be something which has been distasteful to you, some Christian engagement in which you have never been occupied before, may you have grace to say, "Here am I, Lord, send me," whatever the business may happen to be. Ah! what would a church be if it consisted altogether of persons of this sort? What vigor should we have in the Christian army if every soldier felt called to fight! But some of you do not realize your duty in this respect. I would that you would take a farther step. I would that the spirit of service fell upon you, so that you did not merely wear the robe of righteousness but the mantle of service too. Oh! brethren, by the love which

Saw you ruined in the fall,
Yet loved you notwithstanding all,

by the love which gave up its honor and its glory, and took upon itself the form of a servant for your sakes; by the love which sweat great drops of blood in the Garden, by the love which emptied out its heart that you might be redeemed from ruin, I pray you, hear Jesus saying to you, "Follow me"; do follow Him, follow Him in active, industrious, persevering consecration, and from this day forth, if you have hitherto been but a sleeping partner in the great Christian firm, if you have been content to ride upon the Gospel chariot, instead of drawing it or adding an impulse to its wheels, may you say, "My Lord, fill me with the zeal which possessed You; kindle in me the same spirit of service which burned so brightly in Yourself, and as You did call Peter, and Andrew, and James, and John, so do You call me, and say, 'Follow Me.'" You notice, then, that this second call follows the first call, and it is a blessed thing when it does thus succeed and is obeyed.

The Call to Be an Apostle

But in the third text which I gave you, you find Peter called to another service above that of an ordinary worker, that is to say, he is called to be an apostle.

I will venture here to trace an analogy between this and the calling of the Christian minister. You will observe that this call comes last. The call to the apostleship does not come first. Peter is first the catechumen or disciple; secondly, the evangelist; and thirdly, the apostle. So, no man is called to be specially set apart to the ministry of Christ, or to have a share in the apostleship until he has first of all himself known Christ, and until, secondly, as an ordinary Christian he has fully exercised himself in all the duties which are proper to Christian service. Now, some people turn this topsy-turvy. Young men who have never preached are set apart to the ministry, those who have never visited the sick, never instructed the ignorant, and are totally devoid of any knowledge of Gospel experience except the little of their own, are supposed to be dedicated to the Christian ministry. I believe this to be a radical and a fatal error. Brothers and sisters, we have no right to thrust a person into the ministry until he has first given evidence of his own conversion, and has also given proof not only of being a good average worker but something more. If he cannot labor in the church before he pretends to be a minister, he is good for nothing. If he cannot while he is a private member of the church perform all the duties of that position with zeal and energy, and if he is not evidently a consecrated individual while he is a private Christian, certainly you do not feel the guidance of God's Holy Spirit to bid him enter the ministry. No one has a right to aspire to come into that office until, like the knights of old, he has first won his spurs, and has shown that he is really devoted to Christ by having served Him as others have done. Let me say that it would be a very great mercy for this Christian church if some persons would not take this last place at all, but would be content to stop in the second one. There are many people who when set apart to the Christian ministry are a drag and burden to the churches as well as to other people, who if they had but given up themselves as ordinary members to Christian service might have been a very great blessing and honor to the church. One of the kindest pieces of advice I could give to some of our ministerial friends would be, "Go home, and put yourself into some honest way of getting a living; just think whether you were not more serviceable to the church when you were a carpenter or a business person, and when you were earning a considerable sum of money at your own ordinary vocation, than you are now, when you are necessarily dependent upon the gifts and liberality of God's servants without having the ability and the talent which are necessary to make you a leader in the Lord's host." I pray the day may come when we shall all see this, and never think of giving ourselves to the ministry before conversion, and even then aspire not after special work until first of all we have proved that we can serve the Lord in our ordinary lives.

Occasionally I have brethren come to me asking to be received into our college, and one singular reason which some of them give me why they believe that they are called to the ministry is this: "You see, sir, I could not get on at anything else, and therefore I thought Providence must have ordained me to be a minister." I never say a word about that, but I am very clear that if a man is such a fool that he can do nothing else but preach, it is a great pity that he should be allowed to do that; when a brother tells me that, I sometimes venture to ask him if he thinks that God wants the biggest fools to serve Him, whether there should not rather be given up to God's service the very pick, and prime, and flower of the Christian church, those who, if they had addicted themselves to commerce, might have taken the lead therein, or who, if they had given themselves to the bar or to the profession of surgery or medicine, would have stood in the front rank? I believe, friends, we want the strong to take such positions, and that the Lord Jesus Christ has a keen eye, and when He does call someone He calls him to something that he is fit for. Take the cases of Peter and Paul. Peter was a fisherman, it is true, but a fisherman of such a peculiar breed that it would be well if God would find us more of the same sort, who would become fishers of men; and as for Paul, he was one well skilled and learned in all matters, and just fitted and adapted to the work which the Master gave him to do.

The Second Call

I have thus noticed these three calls, but I want now to direct your earnest and particular attention to the second call, because of the lessons to be learned from the character of the men chosen, and the nature of the work entrusted to them.

Character of the Workers

The second call is recorded in the fourth chapter of Matthew and the eighteenth verse; it deserves our attention because we perceive that these brethren were called to the service of Christ while they were engaged in their ordinary vocations.

It seems to have been early in the morning, for Peter was just starting on his work, and was casting his net into the sea; in the twenty-first verse we find that James and John were mending their nets, so that they were all industrious in their ordinary calling. There is a notion abroad among some persons that they cannot serve God unless they neglect their ordinary work. This used to be a complaint brought against the Methodists in the olden time. I believe it was a great falsehood; but it was stated that they were so earnest in listening to sermons that they made bad servants and bad business people. If it was so it was a very grievous fault, but I do not think it ever was the case. However, let none of us fall into it. If I were a Christian and a fisherman, I would like to catch more fish than anybody else. If I were a Christian and a shoeblack, I would desire to clean people's boots so that they shone better than any other shoeblack could make them shine. If I were a Christian employer, I would desire to be the best employer, and if a Christian employee the best employee. Our Christianity, I think, shows itself more, at any rate to the world, in the pursuits of daily life than it does in the engagements of the house of God. "Not forsaking the assembling of ourselves together, as the manner of some is." I scarce need give that exhortation here, but when you do assemble yourselves together, come not up to God's house having the blood of other duties upon your spirits. You are a mother with little children, and it is probably your duty to be at home rather than to be at the prayer meeting. It may sometimes be your business, as a husband, to take turns with your wife and let her come out to the house of God, instead of always taking the privilege yourself. It may be the case with some of you that your business may absolutely require you to be behind the counter both on lecture and on prayer-meeting night, and though I would have you here if possible, and if you do go anywhere go to the house of God, yet do not let it ever be said, or even whispered, that you did not attend to your business, and that you came to grief because the things of God were cared for and your business in consequence neglected. I think it never should be so. I like to recollect that after Jesus Christ had gone away, after He was crucified, died, had been buried, and had risen again, where did He find Peter? Why, He found him fishing again! That is right, Peter. Follow Christ by all manner of means when He bids you, but when there is nothing to do in the service of Christ come back to fishing again. Oh! but some people seem to think that hard work in attending to ordinary business is not spiritual-minded in a Christian. Nonsense! Out with that difficulty, if any of you are troubled by it. Just ask the Lord to clear your brains, and brush away such cobwebs as these, for we shall never have genuine Christianity in the world while such nonsense remains—nonsense about giving up the world, meaning thereby living in laziness! The truest Christian is the working person, who so labors for God that he or she does not neglect the common duties of life. The best form of Christianity is found in the Christian who is a Christian behind the counter, a Christian in the street, a Christian in the marketplace, a Christian anywhere; who, wherever and whenever he or she may be found, is like the Master—"diligent in business, fervent in spirit, serving the Lord."

I think no one will ever serve Christ aright who does not show some energy in other things. I think the Savior chose these four men, not only out of sovereign grace to salvation, but also because He saw about them a zeal in the pursuit of fishery which seemed to mark them out as being the very men to be made useful in His own cause. Notice the character of the men who were thus called to work for Christ; they were active, diligent men, engaged in their own calling. Notice what their occupation was. When Christ called them He said, "You are fishers, and you shall be fishers all your lives; but you are fishers of fish now, and I want you to be fishers of men." He mentions their vocation, and the work He is going to give them. O my brothers and sisters, if you are saved I pray that Jesus may give you that second call, so that you may be earnest "fishers of men"!

Nature of the Work

There is a great deal in that sentence, "fishers of men," a very great deal more than we can bring out now. *A fisherman, you know, must be acquainted with the sea.* Peter knew the Lake of Galilee; I dare say there was not a creek or an inlet in it with which he was not acquainted; he knew the deep places where some kinds of fish were to be found, and the shallow places where others could be caught. And so if you would serve Christ you must know a good deal about people; you must study human nature, and you must watch your opportunities of doing good. You know there are some places where you can meet with more sinners than in others, and there is a certain way of dealing with one disposition, and quite another way of dealing with another. If you are to be a "fisher of men," you must take good stock of the neighborhood where you live. If you would be a "fisher of men" in the Tabernacle, I hope you will know the people near whom you sit, for as you know them, and their pursuits in daily life, and their characters and dispositions, you will be more likely to be blessed, by the help of God's Spirit in bringing them to a knowledge of the truth. A fisherman must be acquainted with the locality where he has to work.

A fisherman must also know how to allure the fish. I saw on Lake Como, when we visited Bellagio, some men fishing. They had torches burning in their boats, and the fish were attracted to them by the glare of the light. You must know how to get the fish together. You know there is such a thing as the ground-bait for the fishes. You must know how to allure people. The preacher does this by using images, symbols, and illustrations. You must know how to catch the fish, throwing out first, perhaps, not a remark directly to the point, because that might be unwise, but a sideways remark, which shall lead to another, and yet another. If you are to be a "fisher of men" you will want your wits about you. It will not do to blunder over people's souls. Fish are not caught by every boy who chooses to take a pin and a piece of cotton and make his way to the pond. Fish want a fisherman, and there is a sort of congruity between the fish and the person who

122 / Classic Sermons on the Apostle Peter

catches them. I do not wonder that Izaak Walton could catch fish. He seems to have been born and made on purpose for it, and so there are some men who are made on purpose for winning souls. They naturally care for their fellows, and they have such a way of putting the truth that as soon as they speak people say, "Here is someone who knows all about me, and knows how to deal with me," and they at once yield to His influence. Oh, that I had hundreds of such in this church! I have a good share of them, and I bless God every time I remember them. God has called them, and has made them true fishers of men; they know about people, and also how to allure them.

The fisherman must be one who can wait with patience. Oh the patience of a fisherman! "We have toiled all night," said the disciples, "and have taken nothing." You cannot be a fisherman unless you are willing to sit and watch, especially if you angle. There you may sit for hours and hours together, and at last when the float begins to move you think you have got your fish, but probably it is only a weed or a frog, and you may watch, and watch, and watch again, and nothing will come of it. Ah! but it is harder work still to wait in Christ's service, to preach twenty times and have no conversions, perhaps to go on teaching in a Sunday school and to see no heartbreaking work done, no sinners crying, "What must I do to be saved?" but to have to go to your knees and say, "Who has believed our report, and to whom is the arm of the Lord revealed?" You will want something within to help you to wait thus; you will want the Holy Spirit of grace Himself dwelling in you to supply you with divine patience, or else you will throw up your work, give away your nets, and say, "I will do something that pays me better than this."

A fisherman, too, is one who must run hazards. Especially was this so on the Lake of Galilee, for that, like many other lakes, was subject to fierce storms. The winds sometimes came rushing down from the mountains, and before the fisherman could take in his sail his boat would be upset. And truly every worker for Christ must expect squalls and stormy weather. Do not think, dear friends, to serve Jesus Christ in those kid gloves and in that nice dainty style of yours. That is not the way in which fish are caught out at sea; it is rough work, and requires someone who can let the wind howl about him without being afraid of his fine curls, or of having the perfume taken out of them. It needs a person that has a bold face and a brave heart, and who when the storm comes looks up to the God of storms, and feels that he is on his Master's service, and may therefore count upon his Master's protection. May the Lord call many members of this church to such work as this, and when the Master shall drag home our net full of big fishes, we shall have a rich reward for all the toils of Christian labor.

The fisherman, once again, *must be one who has learned both how to persevere and how to expect.* The fisherman goes on, and on, and on, and fishes, not sometimes but continually. As Christ's good sower must take the precept, "In the morning sow thy seed, and in the evening withhold not thy hand," so also must His fisherman. "We have toiled all night and taken nothing; nevertheless, at thy command we will let down the net." But I said he must also learn to expect. He must have twinkling in his soul, like a bright particular star, the hope that he shall drag his net to land full of fishes at the last. Beloved, we shall not labor in vain; we shall not spend our strength for naught. We may not live to see the result of the truth which we proclaim, but

> The precious seed shall ne'er be lost,
> For grace ensures the crop.

We must learn to believe in the indestructibility of every truthful testimony, in the immortality of every good deed, in the resurrection of every buried word to live in the sight of God. We must learn to labor and to wait.

There are three words which have been running in my mind for the last few days, and have seemed to work themselves into me, and I hope I may long keep them. One word is *work*, another is *wait*, and the other is *pray*. Work, work, work! Wait, wait, wait! Pray, pray, pray! I think that these three words will enable a person to be, under God, a true and successful fisher of men.

Peter's Response and Ours

I have thus described the sort of men who were called, and the work which Christ gave them to do over and above the work in which they were engaged. I now want you to notice *the prompt obedience* of Peter to this call.

I wonder how it was that Peter came directly Christ said, "Follow me." We know that Peter was a disciple, and consequently, his heart was ready to receive the word which called him to be a servant. It is of no use for me to call some of you to follow Christ, and work for Him as "fishers of men" for if you were to obey, you could not do it acceptably, because you are not the children of God. But you who are saved have something in your hearts that will echo to the exhortation, "Follow me"; I think you need only to have a good work set fairly before you, and to know what it is that the Master requires of you, and you will say at once, "Lord, I will do it," for

'Tis love that makes our cheerful feet
In swift obedience move.

When the heart loves Christ, then the path of duty, which before was rough and rugged, becomes straight and smooth, if not flowery, and the soul says—

Help me to run in thy commands,
'Tis a delightful road;
Nor let my heart, nor feet, nor hands,
Offend against my God.

Beloved friend, very much of the excellence of our service to Christ will depend upon the instantaneous way in which we do it when we know it to be a duty. I believe that debating with oneself about duty is a very dangerous thing. David said, "I made haste, and delayed not to keep thy commandments." Peter did not say, "Lord, let me stop and dry these nets, and hang them up, and bring the boat to shore, and then cast anchor and leave it right," nor did James and John say, "Master, let us go home and kiss that dear mother of ours, and let us see that Zebedee has somebody to take our place"; but immediately they left their nets, and followed Christ. May I urge upon you the habit of falling into the line of duty instantly. When soldiers are being drilled I like to see the way in which the word of command is obeyed the instant it is given. "Right about face!" and the whole line turns right about at once. The thing is done, we say, mechanically. It should be so with us. But I know how it is; we get a right good thought of something we ought to do, but we stop and say, "Now, shall I do it, and when shall I do it?" and for the first hour or two we mean to do it, but by the next day we think it possible that we will decline it, and perhaps when a week is over we give it up altogether. I believe that this is so with many, many Christians in the matter of believers' baptism, to give one instance out of many; they say, "Well, I used to think of it when I was young and I then believed it was my duty, and I think it is my duty now if I really came to consult the Word of God about it, but I have put it off so long; well, perhaps I may see to it one of these days," while there is another and far more likely "perhaps," namely, that having procrastinated so long over that one duty, they will suffer it to go by default. Do not toy with Christian service, friends. There would have been more earnest Whitfields in the world, more Wesleys, more devoted Brainerds and Martyns if men obeyed the call of God instead of taking counsel of flesh and blood, and considering this, that, and the other, and then resolving not to obey. Remember, it is possible for us to have grace in the heart, and yet to be disobedient. We have many such mournful specimens. We cannot but hope that they will enter heaven, for they are washed in the precious blood, and clothed in the Savior's righteousness, but they do little, if anything, for Christ, because they have tampered with His calls, they have violated convictions, and have started back from duties in the exercise of their unbelief, instead of pressing forward in the glory and the majesty of a simple faith in Christ Jesus. If you feel that you have anything to do, do it directly. If God calls you to preach before you go home, do it in the street, I pray you, and if there is anything which claims your immediate attention, if there is a poor person you ought to relieve, if there is anyone to whom you ought to speak before leaving this place, I beseech you do not trifle with the conviction, but as faithful servants of Jesus Christ, being saved, and professing to love Him, I pray you, instantly, to do whatever you feel you ought to do for Him. I have heard of the question being asked in a school, what was the meaning of the text, "Thy will be done on earth as it is in heaven." One said it meant that it should be done truthfully; another, that it should be done unanimously; but a third said it meant that it should be done without asking any questions, and the answer was a good one, for we who do know and love Christ should be willing to do His will without asking any questions.

I must not, however, keep you much longer. I will notice lastly that when the call came to Peter in the shape of "Follow me," *it must have suggested to him many thoughts,* for it contained, in addition to mere service, privilege as well as duty. There was a book written not many years ago by an excellent divine to which I cannot quite subscribe, I mean Dr. Bushnell's *Higher Life.* I cannot subscribe to all that is in it, but I believe that there is a period in the life of some Christians when they rise to a platform elevated above ordinary Christianity, almost as much as ordinary Christianity is elevated above the world. I think that in addition to the first call by which we are brought out of nature's darkness into God's marvelous light, there does come to the Christian, when the Spirit of God works mightily with him, another call by which he is brought into greater familiarity with the Lord Jesus, taught more of conformity to Him in His sufferings, and made to be more fully a partaker of the height and depth and breadth and length of that love which passes all understanding. Such a call seems to me to be imaged in this call of Peter. Have you been living, my dear sister, at a distance from Christ? Have you been obliged to sing the hymn—

'Tis a point I long to know,
Oft it causes anxious thought—
"Do I love the Lord, or no?
Am I his, or am I not?"

I do pray for you, as one of the greatest privileges I could ask God for on your behalf, that Christ may come to you afresh now, and be formed in your heart anew, the hope of glory, in such a way that you may follow Him into close practical fellowship and earnest unstaggering faith. Believe me, it is life to believe in Christ however little, but it is life in health and vigor to believe in Christ with a faith that does not blench. To have Christ and not to see Him is salvation, but to have Him and to see Him is salvation rapturously enjoyed. To be saved and not to know it is a small privilege, but to be saved and to know it, nay, to know Him who is the resurrection and the life and to sit with Him and sup with Him and to feel that His shadow yields a great delight and that His fruit is sweet to one's taste—this is a way of living which angels might almost envy the favored humans who possess it. May the Master call you in that sense now! Pray that prayer which Watts has put into rhyme—

Draw me away from flesh and sense,
One sovereign word shall draw me thence;
I would obey the voice divine,
And all inferior joys resign.

May you get a call from the Master, "Follow Me to the Mount of Transfiguration to see my glory and share in it and abide with me in sacred, rapt, secret fellowship which the world knows nothing of."

This was not merely a call to fellowship, but to practical fellowship. It seemed to say, "Peter, put down your net, and take up the cross; I am to be despised, come and be despised with Me; I am going out of the camp, I shall be scorned and cast out from society; come, Peter, come out of the camp with Me." Oh, may Christ give you such a call as that! You are saved, but still to a great extent you are in the world. Oh, that you might have a separating call—"Come ye out from among them; be ye separate; touch not the unclean thing." May you feel now as if you had gotten a new life over and above the life you have already, that you have fresh blood poured into the veins of your piety that you might rise to something better. Come out and avow your Master; avow Him by nonconformity to the world in all respects.

To conclude. When Christ said, "Follow me," did He not mean that Peter was to follow Him in everything and in all things? May the Master call you and me to follow Him in that consecration to His Father's will which made Him say—"My meat and my drink is to do the will of him that sent me." Oh! there are so many of you professors whose meat and drink are found in trade, or in the making of money, or in the reading of books, or in the study of this and of that. May He call you to make Him the first thing, to make His honor your grand object, and to make His church the true love of your heart reigning in your spirit. Oh! to be wholly given up to Christ, to be a sacrifice upon the altar, smoking, burning, utterly consumed, a living sacrifice, which is your most reasonable service. No, you need not shut up shop; oh, no! but you will go and make money for Christ, and give it to His cause. No, you need not give up your daily labor, but you will be a priest to God even while you are wearing the garments of your trade. No, you must not dare to think of such a thing as withdrawing from your present position, and your little ones round about you, but you must keep where you are, and glorify Christ there, feeling now that you have been called to the work of God, and that that service is to be done just where you are; that you are not to be stargazing and looking aloft for some great thing, but to stand and do a day's work in a day in the sphere where Providence has called you and where grace has blessed you.

Now, you see, I have put all this on the right footing. I have told none of you to serve Christ until you are saved, but when you are saved, I hope and pray that you and I may see Christ calling on us to be "fishers of men."

May the Lord call some who have never been called at all. May it come to pass that this very evening some may look to the Lamb of God dying, bleeding, and suffering. Sinner, He is the Sin-bearer. He came to seek and to save that which was lost. That face was marred with sorrow, and there must you find your hope. Look to Him. That bleeding Man is also the immortal God; trust Him and you are saved. That one act of trust is the means of eternal salvation to everyone that exercises it. Then, being saved may Christ call you, fisherman or whatever you may be, to serve Him until He comes to take you to Himself.

> Teach me, my God and King,
> In all things thee to see;
> And what I do in anything,
> To do it as for thee!
>
> All may of thee partake;
> Nothing so small can be,
> But draws when acted for thy sake,
> Greatness and worth from thee.
>
> If done beneath thy laws,
> E'en servile labors shine;
> Hallowed is toil, if this the cause,
> The meanest work divine.

Peter's Deliverance from Prison

Alexander Maclaren (1826–1910) was one of Great Britain's most famous preachers. While pastoring the Union Chapel, Manchester (1858–1903), he became known as "the prince of expository preachers." Rarely active in denominational or civic affairs, Maclaren invested his time in studying the Word in the original and sharing its truths with others in sermons that are still models of effective expository preaching. He published a number of books of sermons and climaxed his ministry by publishing his monumental *Expositions of Holy Scripture*.

This message is taken from *The Victor's Crowns*, published by Funk and Wagnalls Company (1902).

Alexander Maclaren

10

PETER'S DELIVERANCE FROM PRISON

Peter therefore was kept in prison: but prayer was made
without ceasing of the church unto God for him (Acts 12:5).

THE NARRATIVE OF Peter's miraculous deliverance from
prison is full of little vivid touches which can only have
come from Peter himself. The whole tone of it reminds us
of the Gospel according to St. Mark, which is in like
manner stamped with peculiar minuteness and abundance
of detail. One remembers that at a late period in the life
of the apostle Paul, Mark and Luke were together with
him; no doubt in those days in Rome, Mark, who had
been Peter's special companion and is called by one of the
old Christian writers his "interpreter," was busy in telling
Luke the details about Peter which appear in the first
part of this book of the Acts.

The whole story seems to me to be full of instruction as
well as of picturesque detail; and I desire to bring out the
various lessons which appear to me to lie in it.

The Strength of the Helpless

Look at that eloquent "but" in the verse that I have
taken as a starting point: "Peter therefore was kept in
prison, *but* prayer was made without ceasing of the church
unto God for him." There is another similarly eloquent
"but" at the end of the chapter: "Herod . . . was eaten of
worms, and gave up the spirit, *but* the Word of God grew
and multiplied." Here you get, on the one hand, all the
pompous and elaborate preparations—"four quaternions
of soldiers"—four times four is sixteen—sixteen soldiers,
two chains, three gates with guards at each of them,
Herod's grim determination, the people's malicious expectation of having an execution as a pleasant sensation to

131

wind up the Passover Feast with. And what had the handful of Christian people? Well, they had prayer; and they had Jesus Christ. That was all, and that is more than enough. How ridiculous all the preparation looks when you let the light of that great "but" in upon it! Prayer, "earnest prayer, was made of the church unto God for him." And evidently, from the place in which that fact is stated, it is intended that we should say to ourselves that it was *because* prayer was made for him that what came to pass did come to pass. It is not jerked out as an unconnected incident; it is set in a logical sequence. "Prayer was made without ceasing of the church unto God for him"—and so when Herod would have brought him forth, behold, the angel of the Lord came, and the light shined into the prison. It is the same sequence of thought that occurs in that grand theophany in the eighteenth Psalm, "My cry entered into His ears; then the earth shook and trembled"; and there came all the magnificence of the thunderstorm, and the earthquake, and the divine manifestation; and this was the purpose of it all—"He sent from above, he took me, he drew me out of many waters." The whole energy of the divine nature is set in motion, and comes swooping down from highest heaven to the trembling earth. And of that fact the one end is one poor man's cry, and the other end is his deliverance. The moving spring of the divine manifestation was an individual's prayer; the aim of it was the individual's deliverance. A teaspoonful of water is put into a hydraulic ram at one point, and the outcome is the lifting of tons. So the helpless men and women that can only pray are stronger than Herod and his quaternions and his chains and his gates. "Prayer was made," therefore all that happened was brought to pass, and Peter was delivered.

Peter's companion, James, was killed off, as we read in a verse or two before. Did not the church pray for him? Surely they did. Why was their prayer not answered, then? God has not any step-children. James was as dear to God as Peter was. One prayer was answered; was the other left unanswered? It was the divine purpose that Peter, being prayed for, should be delivered; we may reverently say that if there had not been the many in Mary's house praying, there would have been no angel in Peter's cell.

So here are revealed the strength of the weak, the armor of the unarmed, the defense of the defenseless. If the Christian church in its times of persecution and affliction had kept itself to the one weapon that is allowed it, it would have been more conspicuously victorious. And if we in our individual lives—where, indeed, we have to do something else besides pray—would remember the lesson of that eloquent "but," we should be less frequently brought to perplexity and reduced to something bordering on despair. So my first lesson is the strength of the weak.

The Delay of Deliverance

Peter had been in prison for some days, at any rate, and the praying had been going on all the while, and there was no answer. Day after day "of the unleavened bread" and of the festival was slipping away. The last night had come, "and the same night" the light shone and the angel appeared. Why did Jesus Christ not hear the cry of these poor suppliants sooner? For their sakes; for Peter's sake; for our sakes; for His own sake. For the eventual intervention at the very last moment, and yet at a sufficiently early moment, tested faith. And look how beautifully all bore the test. The man that was to be killed tomorrow is lying quietly sleeping in his cell. Not a very comfortable pillow he had to lay his head upon, with a chain on each arm and a legionary on each side of him. But he slept; while he was asleep Christ was awake, and the brethren and sisters were awake. Their faith was tested, and it stood the test, and thereby was strengthened. And Peter's patience and faith, being tested in like manner and in like manner standing the test, were deepened and confirmed. Depend upon it, he was a better man all his days because he had been brought close up to Death and looked it in the fleshless eye sockets, unwinking and unterrified. And I daresay if long after he had been asked, "Would you not have liked to have escaped those two or three days of suspense, and to have been let go at an earlier moment?" He would have said, "Not for worlds! For I learned in those days that my Lord's time is the best. I learned patience"—a lesson which Peter especially needed—"and I learned trust."

Do you remember another incident, singularly parallel in spirit, though entirely unlike in circumstances, to this one? The two weeping sisters at Bethany send their messenger across the Jordan, grudging every moment that he takes to travel to the far-off spot where Christ is. The message sent is only this: "He whom Thou lovest is sick." What an infinite trust in Christ's heart that form of the message showed! They would not say "Come"; they would not ask Him to do anything; they did not think it was needful; they were quite sure that what He would do would be right.

And how was the message received? "Jesus loved Martha and Mary and Lazarus." Well, did that not make Him hurry as fast as He could to the bedside? No; it rooted Him to the spot. "He abode, *therefore*"—because He loved them—"two days still in the same place where He was," to give him plenty of time to die, and the sisters plenty of time to test their confidence in Him. Their confidence does not seem to have stood the test altogether. "Lord, if Thou hadst been here my brother had not died." "And why wast Thou *not* here?" is implied. Christ's time was the best time. It was better to get a dead brother back to their arms and to their house than that they should never have lost him for those dreary four days. So delay tests faith and makes the deliverance when it comes not only the sweeter, but the more conspicuously divine. So, friends, "men ought always to pray, and not to faint"— ought always to trust that "the Lord will help them, and that right early."

The Leisureliness of the Deliverance

A prisoner escaping might be glad to make a bolt for it, dressed or undressed, anyhow. But when the angel comes into the cell and the light shines, look how slowly and, as I say, leisurely, he goes about it. "Put on your shoes." He had taken them off, with his girdle and his upper garment, that he might lie the less uncomfortably. "Put on your shoes; lace them; make them all right. Never mind about these two legionaries; they will not wake. Gird yourself; tighten your girdle. Put on your garment. Do not be afraid. Do not be in a hurry; there is plenty of time. Now, are you ready? Come." Now it would have been as easy for the angel to have whisked him out of the cell and put him down at Mary's door, but that was not to be the way. Peter was led past all the obstacles—"the first ward," and the soldiers at it; "the second ward," and the soldiers at it; "and the third gate that leads into the city," which was no doubt bolted and barred. There was a leisurely procession through the prison.

Why? Because Omnipotence is never in a hurry and God, not only in His judgments but in His mercies, very often works slowly, as becomes His majesty. "Ye shall not go out with haste; nor go by flight, for the Lord will go before you; and the God of Israel shall be your rereward." We are impatient and hurry our work over; God works slowly, for He works certainly. That is the law of the divine working in all regions; we have to regulate the pace of our eager expectation so as to fall in with the slow, solemn march of the divine purposes, both in regard to our individual salvation and the providences that affect us individually, and in regard to the world's deliverance from the world's evils. "An inheritance may be gotten hastily in the beginning, but the end thereof shall not be blessed." "He that believeth shall not make haste."

The Delivered Prisoner Left to Act for Himself as Soon as Possible

As long as the angel was with him, Peter was dazed and amazed. He did not know—and small blame to him— whether he was sleeping or waking, but he gets through the gates, out into the empty street glimmering in the morning twilight, and the angel disappears, and the slumbering city is lying around him. When he is left to himself, he comes to himself. He could not have passed the wards without a miracle, but he can find his way to Mary's house without one. He needed the angel to bring him as far as the gate and down into the street, but he did not need him any longer. So the angel vanished into the morning light; then he felt himself and steadied himself when responsibility came to him. That is the thing to sober a man. So he stood in the middle of the unpeopled street; "he considered the thing," and found in his own wits sufficient guidance so that he did not miss the angel. He said to himself, "I will go to Mary's house." Probably he did not know that there was anyone praying there, but it was near and it was, no doubt, convenient in other respects that we do not know of. The economy of miraculous power is a remarkable feature in scriptural miracles. God never does anything for us that we could do for ourselves. Not but that our doing for ourselves is in a deeper sense His working on us and in us, but He desires us to take the share that belongs to us in completing the deliverance which must begin by supernatural intervention of one mightier than the angel, even the Lord of angels.

And so this little picture of the angel leading Peter through the prison and then leaving him to his own commonsense and courage as soon as he came out into the street, is just a practical illustration of the great text, "Work out your own salvation with fear and trembling, for it is God that worketh in you."

The Astonishment at the Answer to Their Prayer of the Many Who Pray

They "prayed earnestly"; and when Rhoda was so glad that she left Peter standing out there in the street, in danger of falling into the hands of Herod's men, in order to tell the wonderful story that he was there, the company, when they heard her outpoured narrative, did not believe that their prayer had been answered. They were prepared rather to believe either of two far more unlikely alternatives than to accept the fact that their cry had been heard. In the first place, rather than suppose that it had, they were ready to think that the poor child was mad; then, when that notion was disposed of, they hit on the other hypothesis: "It is his angel." A great many of us have a touch of unbelief in our most earnest petitions and would be surprised at nothing so much as that the answer should stand there before us.

Then come two more of Luke's vivid touches; "Peter continued knocking." No wonder; it was like him, and it was very warrantable in the circumstances that he should persist in hammering at the door while they were discussing inside whether he was there or not. And then it dawned upon some of them that perhaps the best way to settle the debate would be to open the door and see. But this time they do not send Rhoda—perhaps she was too frightened to go back—so we read "*they* opened the door." The whole body of them seem to have flocked out to keep each other in company and courage. "They opened the door, and they were"—what? "Astonished." Then they all began, in Eastern fashion, to talk at once; so Peter "beckoned with his hand to them" to be quiet and did away with the astonishment, for "he told them how the Lord had delivered him."

Well, do not let us pray like them, with unbelief streaking our earnestness and faith. Expect an answer to your prayer; do not be surprised when it comes and do not be ready to adopt any hypothesis, however ridiculous, rather than the plain, Christian one that God has answered your prayer.

"Lord, I believe, help Thou mine unbelief!" said another man whose prayer was a strange mixture of faith and distrust, and Christ helped him. But we are more sure to be helped and to get the answer if we do not doubt, but believe in our hearts that when we stand praying we receive the things that we ask, and then we shall have them.

Christ's Look

Alexander Maclaren (1826–1910) was one of Great
Britain's most famous preachers. While pastoring the
Union Chapel, Manchester (1858–1903), he became known
as "the prince of expository preachers." Rarely active in
denominational or civic affairs, Maclaren invested his time
in studying the Word in the original and sharing its truths
with others in sermons that are still models of effective
expository preaching. He published a number of books of
sermons and climaxed his ministry by publishing his
monumental *Expositions of Holy Scripture*.

This message is taken from *Expositions of Holy
Scripture*, Volume St. Luke 13–24.

Alexander Maclaren

11
CHRIST'S LOOK

And the Lord turned, and looked upon Peter (Luke 22:61).

ALL FOUR EVANGELISTS tell the story of Peter's threefold denial and swift repentance, but we owe the knowledge of this look of Christ's to Luke only. The other Evangelists connect the sudden change in the denier with his hearing the cock crow only, but according to Luke there were two causes cooperating to bring about that sudden repentance, for, he says, "Immediately, while he yet spake, the cock crew. And the Lord turned, and looked upon Peter." And we cannot doubt that it was the Lord's look enforcing the fulfillment of His prediction of the cockcrow that broke down the denier.

Now, it is very difficult, if not impossible, to weave a consecutive whole out of the four versions of the story of Peter's triple denial. But this at least is clear from them all, that Jesus was away at the upper, probably the raised, end of the great hall, and that if any of the three instances of denial took place within that building, it was at such a distance that neither could the words be heard, nor could a look from one end of it to the other have been caught. I think that if we try to localize and picture the whole scene ourselves, we are obliged to suppose that that look, which smote Peter into swift collapse of penitence, came as the Lord Jesus was being led bound down the hall out through the porch, past the fire, and into the gloomy archway on His road to further suffering. As He was thus brought for a moment close to him, "the Lord turned, and looked upon Peter," and then He passed from his sight forever, as he would fear.

I wish, then, to deal—although it must be very imperfectly and inadequately—with that look that changed this man. And I desire to consider two things about it: what it said, and what it did.

What the Look Said

What it said—It spoke of Christ's knowledge, of Christ's pain, of Christ's love.

Of Christ's knowledge—I have already suggested that we cannot suppose that the Prisoner at one end of the hall, intensely occupied with the questionings and argumentation of the priests, and with the false witnesses, could have heard the denial, given in tones subdued by the place, at the other end. Still less could He have heard the denials in louder tones, and accompanied with execrations, which seemed to have been repeated in the porch outside. But as He passed the apostle that look said: "I heard them all—denials and oaths and passion; I heard them all." No wonder that after the Resurrection, Peter, with that remembrance in his mind, fell at the Master's feet and said, "Lord! You know all things. You knew what You did not hear, my muttered recreancy and treason, and my blurted out oaths of denial. You know all things." No wonder that when he stood up among the apostles after the Resurrection and the Ascension and was the mouthpiece of their prayers, remembering this scene as well as other incidents, he began his prayer with "Thou, Lord, which knowest the hearts of all men." But let us remember that this—call it, if you like, supernatural—knowledge which Jesus Christ had of the denial is only one of a great body of facts in His life, if we accept these Gospels, which show that, as one of the Evangelists says at almost the beginning of his history, "He needed not that any man should testify of man, for He knew what was in man." It is precisely on the same line as His first words to Peter, whom He greeted as he came to Him with "Thou art Simon; thou shalt be Cephas." It is entirely on the same line as the words with which He greeted another of this little group, "When thou wast under the fig-tree I saw thee." It is on the same line as the words with which He penetrated to the unspoken thoughts of His churlish entertainer when He said, "Simon! I have somewhat to say unto thee." It is on the lines on which we have to think of that Lord now as knowing us all. He looks still from the judgment seat, where He does not

stand as a criminal, but sits as the supreme and omni-
scient Arbiter of our fates and Judge of our actions. And
He beholds us, each of us, moment by moment as we go
about our work and often by our cowardice, by our faithlessness, by our inconsistencies, "deny the Lord that
bought" us. It is an awful thought, and therefore do men
put it away from them: "Thou God seest me." But it is
stripped of all its awfulness, while it retains all its purify-
ing and quickening power, when we think, as our old
hymn has it:

> Though now ascended up on high,
> He bends on earth a Brother's eye.

And we have not only to feel that the eye that looks
upon us is cognizant of our denials, but that it is an eye
that pities our infirmities and, knowing us altogether,
loves us better than we know. Oh! if we believed in Christ's
look, and that it was the look of infinite love, life would be
less solitary, less sad, and we should feel that wherever
His glance fell there His help was sure, and there were
illumination and blessedness. The look spoke of Christ's
knowledge.

Of Christ's pain—Peter had not thought that he was
hurting his Master by his denials; he only thought of
saving himself. And, perhaps, if it had come into his loving and impulsive nature, which yielded to the temptation the more readily because of the same impulsiveness
which also led it to yield swiftly to good influences, if he
had thought that he was adding another pang to the
pains of his Lord whom he had loved through all his
denial, even his cowardice would have plucked up courage
to "confess, and deny not but confess," that he belonged to
the Christ. But he did not remember all that. And now
there came into his mind—from that look—the bitter
thought, "I have wrung His heart with yet another pang,
and at this supreme moment, when there is so much to
rack and pain Him, I have joined the tormentors."

And so, do we not pain Jesus Christ? Mysterious as it
is, yet it seems as if, since it is true that we please Him
when we are obeying Him, it must be somehow true that

we pain Him when we deny Him, and some kind of shadow of grief may pass even over that glorified nature when we sin against Him and forget Him and repay His love with indifference and reject His counsel. We know that in His earthly life there was no bitterer pang inflicted upon Him than the one which the psalmist prophesied, "He that ate bread with Me hath lifted up his heel against Me." And we know that in the measure in which human nature is purified and perfected, in that measure does it become more susceptible and sensitive to the pain of faithless friends. Chilled love, rejected endeavors to help—which are perhaps the deepest and the most spiritual of sorrows which people can inflict upon one another—Jesus Christ experienced in full measure, heaped up and running over. And we, even we today, may be "grieving the Holy Spirit of God, whereby we are sealed unto the day of redemption." Christ's knowledge of the apostle's denials brought pain to His heart.

Of Christ's love—There was in it saddened disapprobation, but there was not in it any spark of anger, nor what perhaps would be worse, any ice of withdrawal or indifference. But there even at that supreme moment, lied against by false witnesses, insulted and spit upon by rude soldiers, rejected by the priests as an impostor and a blasphemer, and on His road to the cross, when, if ever, He might have been absorbed in Himself, was His heart at leisure from itself, and in divine and calm self-oblivion He could think of helping the poor denier that stood trembling there beneath His glance. That is of a piece with the majestic, yet not repelling, calm which marks the Lord in all His life and which reaches its very climax in the Passion and on the cross. Just as while nailed there He had leisure to think of the penitent thief and of the weeping mother and of the disciple whose loss of his Lord would be compensated by the gaining of her to take care of, so as He was being born to Pilate's judgment, He turned with a love that forgot itself and poured itself into the denier's heart. Is not that a divine and eternal revelation for us? We speak of the love of a brother who, sinned against seventy times seven, yet forgives. We bow in reverence before the love of a mother who cannot forget, but must have compassion on the son of her womb. We wonder at the love of a father who goes out to seek the prodigal. But all these are less than that love which beamed lambent from the eye of Christ as it fell on the denier, and which, in that one transitory glance, revealed for the faith and thankfulness of all ages an eternal fact. That love is steadfast as the heavens, firm as the foundations of the earth. "Yea! the mountains may depart and the hills be removed, but My loving kindness shall not depart, neither shall the covenant of My peace be removed." It cannot be frozen into indifference. It cannot be stirred into heat of anger. It cannot be provoked to withdrawal. Repelled, it returns; sinned against, it forgives; denied, it meekly beams on in self-revelation; it hopes all things, it bears all things. And He who, as He passed out to Pilate's bar, cast His look of love on the denier, is looking upon each of us, if we would believe it, with the same look, pitiful and patient, reproachful and yet forgiving, which unveils all His love, and would fain draw us in answering love to cast ourselves at His feet and tell Him all our sin.

And now, let us turn to the second point that I suggested.

What the Look Did

It tore away the veil that hid Peter's sin from himself. He had not thought that he was doing anything wrong when he denied. He had not thought about anything but saving his own skin. If he had reflected for a moment no doubt he would have found excuses, as we all can do. But when Christ stood there, what had become of the excuses? As by a flash he saw the ugliness of the deed that he himself had done. And there came, no doubt, into his mind in aggravation of the denial all that had passed from that very first day when he had come to Christ's presence, all the confidences that had been given to him, how his wife's mother had been healed, how he himself had been cared for and educated, how he had been honored and distinguished, how he had boasted and vowed and hectored the day before. And so he "went out and wept bitterly."

Now *our* sin captures us by lying to us, by blinding our consciences. You cannot hear the shouts of the people on the bank warning you of your danger when you are in the midst of the rapids, and so our sin deafens us to the still small voice of conscience. But nothing so surely reveals to us the true moral character of any of our actions, be they right or wrong, as bringing them under Christ's eye, and thinking to ourselves, "Dare I do that if He stand there beside me and see it?" Peter could deny Him when He was at the far end of the hall. He could not have denied Him if he had had Him by his side. And if we will take our actions, especially any of them about which we are in doubt, into His presence, then it will be wonderful how conscience will be enlightened and quickened, how the Fiend will start up in his own shape, and how poor and small the motives which tempted so strongly to do wrong will come to look when we think of adducing them to Jesus. What did a maidservant's flippant tongue matter to Peter then? And how wretchedly inadequate the reason for his denial looked when Christ's eye fell upon him. The most recent surgical method of treating skin diseases is to bring an electric light, ten times as strong as the brightest street lights, to bear upon the diseased patch, and fifty minutes of that searchlight clears away the disease. Bring the beam from Christ's eye to bear on your lives and you will see a great deal of leprosy and scurf and of lupus, and all that you see will be cleared away. The look tore down the veil.

It melted the denier's heart into sorrow. I can quite understand a conscience being so enlightened as to be convinced of the evil of a certain course, and yet there being none of that melting into sorrow, which, as I believe, is absolutely necessary for any permanent victory over sins. No one will ever conquer his evil as long as he only shudderingly recoils from it. He has to be broken down into the penitential mood before he will secure the victory over his sin. You remember the profound words in our Lord's pregnant parable of the sower, how one class which transitorily was Christian had for its characteristic that immediately with joy they received the word. Yes; a Christianity that puts repentance into a parenthesis and talks about faith only, will never underlie a permanent and thorough reformation. There is nothing that brings "godly sorrow" so surely as a glimpse of Christ's love; nothing that reveals the love so certainly as the "look." You may hammer at someone's heart with law, principle, and moral duty, and all the rest of it, and you may get him to feel that he is a very poor creature, but unless the sunshine of Christ's love shines down upon him there will be no melting; if there is no melting there will be no permanent bettering.

It kept the sorrow from turning into despair. Judas "went out and hanged himself." Peter "went out and wept bitterly." What made the one the victim of remorse, and the other the glad child of repentance? How was it that the one was stiffened into despair that had no tears, and the other was saved because he could weep? Because the one saw his sin in the lurid light of an awakened conscience, and the other saw his sin in the loving look of a pardoning Lord. And that is how you and I ought to see our sins. Be sure, dear friend, that the same long-suffering, patient love is looking down upon each of us, and that if we will, like Peter, let the look melt us into penitent self-distrust and heart-sorrow for our clinging sins, then Jesus will do for us as He did for that penitent denier on the Resurrection morning. He will take us away by ourselves and speak healing words of forgiveness and reconciliation so that we, like him, will dare in spite of our faithlessness to fall at His feet and say, "Lord, You know all things; You know that I, earlier faithless and treacherous, love You; and all the more because You have forgiven the denial and restored the denier."

Peter's Protest

Henry Parry Liddon (1829–1890) belonged to the High
Church school of the Anglican Church. Ordained in 1853,
he served in two brief pastorates and as vice principal of a
school. He moved to Oxford and there preached to large
crowds at St. Mary's and Christ Church. He is perhaps
best known for his Bampton Lectures, *The Divinity of
Our Lord and Savior Jesus Christ.* From 1870 to his death,
he was canon of St. Paul's Cathedral, London, which he
sought to make into an Anglican preaching center to rival
Charles Spurgeon's Metropolitan Tabernacle.

    This sermon is taken from *Sermons by H. P. Liddon* in
the Contemporary Pulpit Library, Volume 3, published by
Swan Sonnenschein & Co., London, 1891.

H. P. Liddon

12

PETER'S PROTEST

Peter answered and said unto him, Though all men shall
be offended because of thee, yet will I never be offended
(Matthew 26:33).

NO OTHER APOSTLE makes us feel so much at home with
him as Peter. He is one of the three or four of whom we
know most. John, of course, the beloved disciple, has a
great place in our hearts, but then we know that his
relationship to our Lord is unique. Paul's labors are so
abundant, his place in the New Testament is so
commanding, that we see and hear more of him than of
any other apostle, but then he is as much beyond us in
his work as is John in his love. The two apostles James,
the first martyred apostle and the first cousin of the Lord,
august and beautiful figures as they are, are more in the
background: we see them far less distinctly. Peter indeed
in point of rank is, as Matthew expressly says, the first
apostle, and yet this does not destroy our sense of
fellowship with his personal character: he has—if it be
not irreverent to say so—he has so much in common with
us; he so draws us to him by his humanity, by his
eagerness, by his impetuosity, by his enthusiasm—nay,
by his weakness, by his rashness, by his buoyancy, by his
self-reproving penitence. And we feel all this especially in
the pathetic scene which is described in the second lesson
for this afternoon.

The Holy Sacrament had just been instituted; the disciples had sung the hymn of thanksgiving, and they had
gone out to the Mount of Olives, and Peter ventured to
ask the question, "Whither goest thou?" It was in Peter
the language of anxious love, and our Lord answered it by
saying that Peter, though still unprepared, would yet in
the end follow Him. And then Peter made his first protest

of unfailing loyalty, and our Lord first predicted his coming fall. A second protestation and a second warning is described in the text. Our Lord had mercifully granted to warn the apostles that they were on the eve of a scene which had been described in prophecy. Then said Jesus to them, "All ye shall be offended because of me this night: for it is written, I will smite the shepherd, and the sheep of the flock shall be scattered abroad." The prophecy is from Zechariah, but our Lord employs a word which recalls another and a sterner prophecy in Isaiah. It is that in which Israel was warned that the Lord would one day become to Israel a stone of stumbling and a rock of offense; Paul, as we know, tells the Romans that this was fulfilled when in the later days of the apostles the majority of the Jewish people deliberately rejected Jesus as the true Messiah. But to be offended at God or His representative was a crime and a misery from which good Jews shrank back with terror, so that when our Lord used this word describing what would presently be the conduct of His own disciples, the prediction roused Peter once more to make a counter-protest, that whatever might be the case with others, he at least would answer for himself: "Though all men should be offended because of thee, yet will I never be offended." He soon had occasion to discover how far he had meant his words. He was chosen to witness the agony in Gethsemane along with James and John. He stood by while his Master was arrested. He followed our Lord to the house of the high priest, and there, as he sat in the outer hall among the servants and the many waiting there, his trial came on him, but found him unprepared. Thrice he was challenged; thrice, and the last time with passionate vehemence, he denied his Master, and when our Lord turned and looked upon Peter, that glance recalled the words, "Though all men should be offended because of thee, yet will I never be offended."

The Confidence of Inexperience

Now one reason of Peter's overconfidence was that he did not realize the situation which was awaiting him. As yet he had had no experience of any trial of the kind, and he seems not to have had that kind of imagination which can anticipate the untried with any sort of accuracy. When he said, "Though all men should be offended because of Thee, yet will I never be offended," he had not thought out in detail what was meant by the contingency which he thus describes. He had never yet seen his Master deserted by His friends and disciples, and he really treats such an occurrence in his inmost heart as utterly improbable. It is for him so improbable that he can afford to say without much reflection what he would do if it arose. He refers to it with that absence of entire seriousness with which men sometimes proclaim publicly how they would act if they were to find themselves in positions which they are not likely in any event to occupy. And thus civilians argue at length and with warmth as to the best way of handling Her Majesty's forces in the field; thus writers for the press explain how, if they were bishops, they would steer the church through existing controversies. All such persons express themselves with freedom, and even with audacity, because they never look forward to be put to the proof. If they had to discuss great affairs as those who are actually responsible for their conduct, they would be no doubt much less emphatic and striking in what they say; but, at the same time, they would be much wiser. They would think out the situation in all its bearings, and this patient thorough travail of thought would produce in them a salutary hesitation.

Had Peter placed clearly before his mind what was meant by all being offended at Christ, had he pictured to himself how matters would stand when even James, even John had forsaken the divine Master, he would have shrunk from adding his concluding words, or at least he would have turned them into a prayer: "Grant, Lord, that I in my sin and my weakness may not be offended at You."

Peter's confidence was then first of all the confidence of inexperience, aided by lack of imagination. It is repeated again and again under our eyes at the present day. Castles in the air are built by inexperienced virtue, to be demolished, alas! at the first touch of the realities of vice. The country lad who has been brought up in a Christian home, and is coming up to some great business house in London makes vigorous protestations of what he will and will not do in a sphere of life of the surroundings of which he can as yet form no true idea whatever. The emigrant who is looking forward to spend his days in a young colony where the whole apparatus of Christian and civilized life is yet in its infancy, or is altogether wanting, makes plans leaving the surroundings of a situation, of which he cannot at all as yet from the nature of the case take the measure, altogether out of account. The candidate for holy orders who anticipates his responsibilities from afar, gathering them from books, gathering them from occasional interaction with clergymen, makes resolutions which he finds have to be revised by the light of altogether unforeseen experiences. Peter never knew what it was to be the only human being loyal to Christ until he sat in that outer court of the high priest's palace, and the terrible isolation was too much for him. All were indeed then in that tragic moment—all were offended at his Lord, and after a struggle he, *he* too was offended.

The Confidence of Self-reliance

And closely allied to this general failure to realize an untried set of circumstances was Peter's insufficient sense at this period of his life of the possibly awful power of an entirely new form of temptation. He had as yet, it might seem, had no very great trial to undergo. After giving up his own calling as a fisherman to follow our Savior, he had, like the rest, been kept privily in His presence from the provoking of all men; he had accompanied our Lord in His journeys; he had witnessed the healing of his own mother-in-law in his own house; he had been one of the three selected witnesses of the raising of Jairus' daughter; he had been placed at the head of the list of the apostles who were chosen from among the body of disciples to wait specially on the person of our Lord, and who were endowed with higher powers than nature could give them in order to enable them to spread His kingdom among men.

He had, on two occasions especially, shown a devotion
to our Lord and an insight into His real claims and
character which were not at the time shared by the other
apostles. When our Lord preached in the great synagogue
of Capernaum and taught how hereafter men should live
by eating and drinking His body and blood in the sacrament of the Holy Communion, many of the disciples took
offense and deserted Him, and Jesus said to the Twelve,
"Will ye also go away?" And at once Peter became the
spokesman of the rest. "Lord, to whom shall we go? Thou
hast the words of eternal life, and we believe and are sure
that thou art the Christ, the Son of the living God." And
again at Caesarea Philippi, when our Lord asked the
Twelve, on their return from their first missionary enter-
prise, whom they as distinct from the populace in general
said that He was, Peter stepped forward with the confession, "Thou art the Christ, the Son of the living God"; and
he was rewarded by the great blessing which was fulfilled
by his personal labors immediately after the day of Pentecost: "I say unto thee that thou art Peter, and upon this
rock I will build my church, and the gates of hell shall not
prevail against it."

If we find in Peter's earlier history elements of a different kind; if his remonstrance with our Lord, who had
foretold His own humiliation and death, was even pre-
sumptuous; if he was, as it might seem, almost bewildered on the Mount of the Transfiguration; if his question,
"How far shall my brother sin against me and I forgive
him?" shows that he had not yet learned the true moral
meaning of the Gospel law; if his sinking in the water
when he had left the ship to go to Jesus implies partial
failure of faith; if his question, "We have left all and followed Thee, what shall we have therefore?" betrays a lack
of perfect disinterestedness—still, the great confessions
at Capernaum and at Caesarea Philippi—these were key-
notes, these were the ruling principles of his life, and they
might have seemed to make it certain that he could trust
himself never to be offended.

Of what actually happened to Peter we may see instances enough in history or in daily life. A man living in

a comparatively obscure position is exemplary; his little failures do but serve to set forth the sterling worth of his general character. He seems to be marked out for some promotion; his friends predict, all the world predicts, that he will be a great success since he has shown on a small scale excellencies which will certainly distinguish him and will adorn a larger sphere. He is promoted, and he turns out a hopeless failure. "How extraordinary!" cries out the world. "Who could have anticipated it?" exclaim his friends. And yet the explanation may be a very simple one. He may have been by the change of circumstances for the first time in his life put under the influence of a temptation hitherto unknown to him. He may have been tempted in his earlier years by appeals to avarice, by appeals to illicit desire, by appeals to personal vanity, but never, never as yet to the pressure of the fear of man. In that place of prominence he for the first time feels the fear of a mass of human opinion which he does not in his conscience and in his heart respect, but which he fears only because it is a mass. And this fear is too much for him, too much for his sense of justice, for his charity, for his consistency with his former self. Alas! that new temptation has found out a weak place in his moral nature, it has sprung a leak in him, and the disappointment is as keen today as his expectations of yesterday were unduly sanguine.

Capax imperii nisi imperasset—an admirable emperor if he only had never reigned—was the historian's saying about one of the rulers of the ancient world; this is true of many a man who, after years of good conduct, are placed for the first time in life under the play and stress of an entirely new temptation. So it was with Peter. He sat down in the outer hall to see the end, and then came the side glancings and the rising suspicions of discipleship, and the partial identifications and the long whispered conjectures, and the openly uttered fierce remarks, and the vehement assertions, each one more positive than the preceding, "This man also was with Jesus of Nazareth"; "Surely thou also art one of them, for thy speech betrayeth thee"; and behind all this was the accumulated fund of deep, implacable, angry passion that filled the hearts of the Jewish people, and that was bent upon its projects of vengeance with all the apparatus of mock justice and swift torture and execution at its disposal; Peter's heart sank within him. Here was a motive, the power of which he had never experienced, never suspected.

The Confidence of Natural Temperament

And once more Peter's overconfidence would seem to have been due in part to his natural temperament and to his reliance on it. Impetuosity was the basis of his character; it had stood him in good stead; it had no doubt been strengthened by exercise during his earlier years as a fisherman of the Galilean lake. God's grace does not destroy the natural character; it purifies, it raises, it sanctifies character. Peter's nature took a new direction after his conversion to Christ, but its main features, its substance, its stock, remained as before—hopeful, eager, sanguine, impetuous. While grace is trustworthy in time of trial, nature, as many of us know, may be expected to give way. This confusion between grace and nature has constantly occurred in the history of Christendom. One great instance of it is noteworthy in the enthusiasm which led to the Crusades. No well-informed and fair-minded person can question the genuine love of our lord Jesus Christ which filled such men as Peter the Hermit, and still more that great preacher and writer Bernard. These men exerted an influence some seven centuries ago upon the populace of central Europe to which the modern world affords absolutely no parallel, and at their voices thousands of men in all ranks of life left their homes to rescue, if it might be, from the hands of the infidel the sacred soil on which the Redeemer had lived and died. So they filled the fortresses, the warriors of those days; and who can doubt that of these not a few were animated by a motive which is always noble—that of giving the best they had to give, their very lives, to the God who had made and redeemed them? But also who can doubt that many, perhaps the large multitude, were really impelled by very different considerations which gathered round this central idea,

and seemed to receive from it some sort of consecration
that a love of adventure, a love of reputation, a desire to
escape from troubled times at home, the hope of influence
or power that might be of use elsewhere than in Palestine
that might make a family name, that might found or
consolidate a dynasty—also entered into the sum of moral
forces which precipitated the crusading hosts on the coasts
of Syria?

Another instance is observable in the manner in which,
even in our own day, a great many persons hold what is
called the theory of assurance. If you have an assurance
that you are saved, then you are saved. If you do not feel
this assurance, then you are not saved. Yet how precari-
ous, how untrustworthy is the ground on which that theory
proceeds! A robust physical temperament will sometimes
issue in that very frame of easy confidence toward God
which is called, far too lightly, spiritual assurance; and
gentle, tender, sensitive consciences, who are overpow-
ered by the sense of their own deficiencies, without being
at all insensible to the greatness of our Savior's redeeming love, cannot attain to this easy and confident and
offhand frame of mind, do what they will. Is it certain,
think you, that in the eyes of Him who sees us as we are
the man of robust self-confidence is saved, and the man of
hesitating, reverent self-distrust is lost? Is it certain that
the first exhibits only the strength and majesty of God's
grace, and the second only the weakness and faithlessness of unregenerate nature? Assurance is a spiritual
thing, not a matter of temperament, and it is never divorced from the conviction that, as while there is life hope
is always possible, so, on the other hand, while probation
lasts there must be always at least the possibility of failure. Even Paul expresses his anxiety "lest that by any
means when I have preached to others, I myself should be
a castaway." Certainly we cannot think too highly of the
great gift of perseverance. The Bible is full of it from the
psalmist to John. It *is* a great gift; and, instead of assum-
ing that it has been certainly given to us, we would do
well to pray for it. Prayer is safe for such people as you
and I—safer than expressions of confidence as to what we

are, and as to what we shall be, even though we acknowledge that it is only the grace of God which makes us what
we are.

The Lesson

What, then, is the lesson which we are to try to carry
away from this one point in Peter's history? Not, assuredly, to think cheaply of moral and religious enthusiasm. Enthusiasm is the glow of the soul, the lever by
which people are raised above their average level and
become capable of a goodness and a benevolence which
but for it would be impossible. The soul, like nature, has
its revenge sooner or later on all pedantic one-sidedness.
If enthusiasm is expelled from the life of one generation,
it reappears in that of the next. The last century did not
gain much by depreciating it: that age of cold, clear reason, as it fancied itself to be, was closed, at least on the
continent, by a tempest of irrational passion without a
parallel in the history of the world. But what this episode really teaches us is to measure well, if possible, our
religious language, especially the language of fervor and
devotion. When the sons of Zebedee asked through their
mother to sit the one on Christ's right hand and the
other on His left in His kingdom, He checked aspirations
the true import of which they had not weighed. When
the young man came to Him with the question, "Good
Master, what shall I do to inherit eternal life?" our Lord
saw that he was using language which he did not mean,
and that he had no idea as to who it was to whom he
thus lightly paid a conventional compliment. "Why callest
thou me good?" And so, again, our Lord contrasts the
servant who said, "I go, sir!" and went not, with the
servant who made no profession of obedience, and yet
went. When religious language outruns practice or conviction, the general character is weakened; it is weakened by any insincerity; it is especially weakened by
insincerity addressed to the All-true. Let us be sparing
of free professions of our own. Especially let us, in the
words of today's Collect, "pray Him from whose only gift
it cometh, that His faithful people do unto Him true and

laudable service, to enable us so faithfully to serve Him in this life, even to the end that when its trials are over we fail not finally to attain His heavenly promises, through Jesus Christ our Lord."

Sermon resources for your reading enrichment!

Reading these sermons will enrich your life and enhance your skills as an interpreter, teacher, and communicator of God's truth.

Classic Sermons on the Apostle Peter
ISBN 0-8254-3998-1   160 pp.   paperback

Classic Sermons on the Attributes of God
ISBN 0-8254-4038-6   160 pp.   paperback

Classic Sermons on the Birth of Christ
ISBN 0-8254-4044-0   160 pp.   paperback

Classic Sermons on Christian Service
ISBN 0-8254-4041-6   160 pp.   paperback

Classic Sermons on the Cross of Christ
ISBN 0-8254-4040-8   160 pp.   paperback

Classic Sermons on Faith and Doubt
ISBN 0-8254-4028-9   160 pp.   paperback

Classic Sermons on Family and Home
ISBN 0-8254-4054-8   160 pp.   paperback

Classic Sermons on Heaven and Hell
ISBN 0-8254-3995-7   160 pp.   paperback

Classic Sermons on Hope
ISBN 0-8254-4045-9   160 pp.   paperback

Classic Sermons on the Miracles of Jesus
ISBN 0-8254-3999-x   160 pp.   paperback

Classic Sermons on the Names of God
ISBN 0-8254-4052-1   160 pp.   paperback

Classic Sermons on Overcoming Fear
ISBN 0-8254-4043-2   160 pp.   paperback

Classic Sermons on Praise
ISBN 0-8254-3994-9   160 pp.   paperback

Classic Sermons on Prayer
ISBN 0-8254-4029-7   160 pp.   paperback

Classic Sermons on the Prodigal Son
ISBN 0-8254-4039-4   160 pp.   paperback

Classic Sermons on the Resurrection of Christ
ISBN 0-8254-4042-4   160 pp.   paperback

Classic Sermons on the Second Coming and Other Prophetic Themes
ISBN 0-8254-4051-3   160 pp.   paperback

Classic Sermons on the Sovereignty of God
ISBN 0-8254-4055-6   160 pp.   paperback

Classic Sermons on Spiritual Warfare
ISBN 0-8254-4049-1   160 pp.   paperback

Classic Sermons on Suffering
ISBN 0-8254-4027-0   208 pp.   paperback

Classic Sermons on Worship
ISBN 0-8254-4037-8   160 pp.   paperback

Treasury of the World's Great Sermons

One hundred and twenty-three sermons by many of the world's most notable preachers of ancient and modern times, compiled by Warren W. Wiersbe.

A sermon library in one volume!

Great pulpit princes and their sermon masterpieces are organized and presented together with brief biographies, along with indexes of authors, sermon topics, and Bible texts. Together they illustrate a variety of gifts and diversity of methods along with national and ecclesiastical peculiarities.

This list of great preachers includes theologians such as John Calvin and Jonathan Edwards; evangelists such as Christmas Evans; and pulpiteers such as Charles H. Spurgeon, G. Campbell Morgan, and Alexander Maclaren.

Although each one is representative of the preaching that characterized the age to which it belongs, each sermon contains a distinct message helpful in solving present-day problems in Christian living as well as literary and rhetorical excellence.

"Every minister should be a reader," writes Warren W. Wiersbe. Himself an ardent reader of sermons and biographies, he recommends that every minister read the giants—the great writers and preachers of all centuries—both what they have written and their biographies.

For variety and solid content, *The Treasury of the World's Great Sermons* is a classic sermon resource for every pastor's library.

ISBN 0-8254-4002-5   672 pp.   paperback

Available from your local Christian bookstore, or

P.O. Box 2607, Grand Rapids, MI 49501

DATE DUE